HIDDEN SIGNS IN THE OLIVET DISCOURSE

Hidden Signs in the Olivet Discourse
Copyright ©2005 by Midnight Call Ministries
Published by The Olive Press a subsidiary of Midnight Call Inc.
Columbia, South Carolina, 29228

Copy Typist: Lynn Jeffcoat
Copy Editor: Susanna Cancassi
Proofreaders: Angie Peters, Susanna Cancassi
Layout/Design: Michelle Kim, Lisa Howell
Lithography: Simon Froese
Cover Design: Michelle Kim

Library of Congress Cataloging-in-Publication Data

Lieth, Norbert
    Hidden Signs in the Olivet Discourse
    ISBN #0-937422-62-2

    1. Prophecy   2.Bible Teaching   3. Christian Living

Printed in the United States of America

The sole purpose of publishing this book is to encourage the reader to surrender and consecrate his life to Jesus Christ.

All funds received from the sale of this book will be used exclusively for the furtherance of the Gospel.

No one associated with this ministry receives a royalty for any of the literature published by Midnight Call Ministries, Inc.

Contents

Introduction

The Olivet Discourse took place only a few days prior to Jesus' death. It is one of the most important prophetic speeches in Scripture. All further revelations on this subject — right up to the last book of the Bible — are founded upon this endtime speech. Jesus gave it to us as a "testament of hope," so to speak.

Hours before His death, the Lord kept the Feast of the Passover and instituted the first Holy Communion with His disciples, therewith initiating the New Covenant with His blood. In reference to this, the Apostle Paul wrote: "For as often as ye eat this bread, and drink this cup, ye do shew the Lord's death till he come" (1 Corinthians 11:26). Jesus spoke with His own about His return and the events in connection with it. This same Mount of Olives will ultimately be the location of His return in glory (compare Zechariah 14:4).

The Olivet Discourse teaches us how we can order the coming events and pass on information concerning them. We are encouraged to reach those outside with the Gospel as we continue in our personal sanctification. We are admonished not to sink in the depression of the world but to hold up the hope of His return.

The Lord will return in the clouds of heaven with great power and glory (Matthew 24:30). This is the ultimate goal of all prophecies concerning the future of Israel, the Church and the nations.

When we see the chaos taking place today in the Middle East, the perplexity of the nations, and the confusion within Christianity, we are glad and grateful that the Lord left us this message on the Mount of Olives. It comforts us to know that everything has to come as He said, that the Lord has everything in His control, and that ultimately — soon, we hope! — the heavens will open up, from which Jesus will appear. Sincere Christians may be encouraged that the Lord will return with His Church, which was raptured beforehand, to begin His reign of righteousness (2 Thessalonians 1:7).

In this exegesis of the Olivet Discourse I was concerned, among other things, with the specific time the Lord referred to. It particularly concerns Israel, the events of the Great Tribulation, which precede His return in great power and glory, and not the Church or the Rapture. Many things, however, can be applied spiritually to the Church, and I have attempted to do this wherever possible.

–Norbert Lieth

Chapter 1

THREE QUESTIONS ABOUT THE END OF THE AGE

No question concerning Jerusalem is more important than the one the disciples asked in the following text. We are concerned with the partition of Jerusalem, what the city's future looks like, and what will become of it politically. God answered this question long ago.

"And Jesus went out, and departed from the temple: and his disciples came to him for to shew him the buildings of the temple. And Jesus said unto them, See ye not all these things? Verily I say unto you, There shall not be left here one stone upon another, that shall not be thrown down. And as he sat upon the mount of Olives, the disciples came unto him privately, saying, Tell us, when shall these things be? And what shall be the sign of thy coming, and of the end of the world?" (Matthew 24:1-3). The New International Version translates "end of the world" as "the end of the age."

The Lord Jesus spoke about Jerusalem's imminent destruction in Matthew 23:37-38, then in verse 39, He said: "Ye shall not see me henceforth, till ye shall say, Blessed is he that cometh in the name of the Lord."

Jerusalem was Judaism, the city of the great King (Matthew 5:35). This was where God revealed Himself on numerous occasions through His prophets and messengers, and it was the place where He sent His only Son (Matthew 21:37). This city has always represented Israel. But in this city, the authorities were about to reject the greatest offer of God's love (John 1:11). They rejected the promised Son of David and did not want Him to reign over them (Luke 19:14, 27). They were even prepared to nail Him to the cross.

That is the bitter truth concerning Israel at that time. The Lord had no message for Israel besides one of judgment: "Behold, your house is left unto you desolate" (Matthew 23:38). The visible sign the Lord gave was that He left the temple ("And Jesus went out, and departed from the temple" [Matthew 24:1]) and did not return. The house of Israel was already desolate; His departure would reap terrible consequences. Jerusalem missed its chance for refuge under the shadow of God's wings. All that remained was a desert that offered no shade. With His statement in Matthew 23:37, the Lord Jesus gave one of the last and most tremendous revelations of His person: "O Jerusalem, Jerusalem, thou that killest the prophets, and stonest them which are sent unto thee, how often would I have gathered thy children together, even as a hen gathereth her chickens under her wings, and ye would not!" Who was speaking here? Jesus surely said this with Psalm 91:1-4 in mind: "He that dwelleth in the secret place of the most High shall abide under the shadow of the Almighty. I will say of the LORD, He is my refuge and my fortress: **my God**: in him will I trust. Surely he shall deliver thee from the snare of the fowler, and from the noisome pestilence. He shall cover thee with his feathers, and under his wings shalt thou trust: his truth shall be thy shield and buckler" (compare also Psalm 57:2). Jesus' words recorded at the end of Matthew 23 stated, in effect, "I am God, your God, the God of Abraham, Isaac and Jacob, but you do not want Me!"

Tremendous about this is that the Lord looked beyond these words describing His judgment, His death, the dispersion of Israel, and the Great Tribulation, and turned the spotlight to His ultimate return for the Jewish people: "For I say unto you, Ye shall not see me henceforth, till ye shall say, Blessed is he that cometh in the name of the Lord" (Matthew 23:39). Jesus pointed to the end of the tunnel as He prophetically saw the remnant of Jews who will await the Lord. They will recognize Him as the One they pierced. The Lord had said this through David in the words of Psalm 118:26-27: "Blessed be he that cometh in the name of the LORD: we have blessed you out of the house of the LORD. God is the LORD, which hath shewed us light."

It will be a long and difficult path until Israel's cry is heard at Jesus' return, which He described in chapters 24 and 25.

We must assume that Jesus' disciples heard what He had said regarding Jerusalem and the temple. Certainly they were in consternation, for they could not or did not want to accept the proclamation of their destruction. That is why Scripture states: "And Jesus went out, and departed from the temple: and his disciples came to him for to shew him the buildings of the temple" (Matthew 24:1). Mark's account of this event says, "And as he went out of the temple, one of his disciples saith unto him, Master, see what manner of stones and what buildings are here!" (Mark 13:1). In other words, "This place cannot become desolate; it is the house of God!" But instead of agreeing with His disciples, the Lord added to His

14

words of judgment: "See ye not all these things? Verily I say unto you, There shall not be left here one stone upon another, that shall not be thrown down" (Matthew 24:2).

The Disciples Asked Three Questions

Following the proclamation of the temple's complete destruction, the disciples asked the Lord Jesus three questions:

1. "Tell us, when shall these things be?" (Matthew 24:3). They asked Him this question in connection with the destruction of the temple and of Jerusalem. But because they were believing Jews who also believed in the establishment of the Messianic kingdom, and because the Lord Himself had spoken of His return (Matthew 23:39), their next questions were,

2. "and what shall be the sign of thy coming?"

3. "and of the end of the world"[age]?

The last two questions can actually be regarded as one.

Jesus' Audience

Because the Church was still a mystery at that time, we can conclude that it could not have been the object of the Lord's statements in Matthew 24. (Remember, the Church was not introduced until Pentecost, and was later revealed by Paul.) The Jews were the primary group addressed; we know this from the context: "Jerusalem, Jerusalem…your house

15

[the temple] is left unto you desolate...Ye shall not see me henceforth, till ye shall say, Blessed is he that cometh in the name of the Lord" (Matthew 23:37-39).

This "coming" mentioned by Christ in that passage does not refer to the Rapture, but to His return in great power and glory for the Jews following the Great Tribulation (Matthew 24:29-31). It wasn't until later, shortly before Gethsemane, that the Lord spoke about the Rapture (compare John 14:1ff). Until then the Jewish disciples only knew about the glorious coming age of the Messiah (compare, for instance with Luke 17:22-37).

The disciples to whom the Lord was speaking, whom we must clearly consider as being Jewish, prophetically represent the Messianic-believing remnant at the time of the Great Tribulation (compare footnote concerning Matthew 10:23 in the Scofield Bible).

Jesus' Message

The Lord, in His Olivet Discourse, described the Jewish situation immediately before His return.

False Christs, False Prophets

One point He stressed was that false prophets or christs (Matthew 24:5, 23-24) would be a danger for Israel. Because of His warning, the Church has to beware of false teachers, false apostles and false evangelists, and must learn to test the spirits (2

Corinthians 11:13; 2 Peter 2:1; Galatians 1:6-9 and 1 John 4:1). The false prophet will come "out of the earth" (Revelation 13:11), which points to Israel, in contrast to "out of the sea" (Revelation 13:1), which points to the nations.

Children of God who have been born again of the Holy Spirit and who belong to the New Covenant will certainly not fall prey to the kinds of deceptions described in Matthew 24:5, 23-24. Israel, not the Church of Jesus Christ, needs to fear a false Christ. The Jewish people are waiting for an earthly Messiah as far as their restoration is concerned. They have been deceived regarding this earthly Messiah many times already. For instance, many believed Rabbi von Lubavitch Menachem Mendel Schneerson, who died in 1994, was the long-awaited Messiah. Even while he was on his deathbed, hundreds of Hassidic Jews danced and sang, "Long live our lord and rabbi, the Messiah-King." [1]

Concerning the coming false messiah, Jesus said: "if another shall come in his own name, him ye will receive" (John 5:43). He prophesied of His own return: "For as the lightning cometh out of the east, and shineth even unto the west; so shall also the coming of the Son of man be" (Matthew 24:27). His appearance cannot and will not be overlooked (verse 30).

Abomination of Desolation

The abomination of desolation (Matthew 24:15) clearly refers to the Jewish land, the Jewish temple and the Jewish sacrifice. Daniel the prophet wrote about the prophetic event in Daniel 9:27. The angel Gabriel did not speak to Daniel concerning the 70 weeks of years of the Church of Jesus Christ, but told him that they were "determined upon thy people and upon thy holy city" (verse 24).

The verse, "Then let them which be in Judea flee into the mountains" (Matthew 24:16), speaks for itself. The Jewish land is meant here. The New Testament does not say that we are to flee to the mountains. (The same is true about the Sabbath written about in Matthew 24:20, which is meant for Judaism and has nothing to do with Christianity.) The parable of the fig tree in verse 32 also offers a picture of the Jewish nation, and the Lord's statement concerning the "generation" in verse 34 also refers to Israel.

Jesus' Time Frame

"But he that shall endure unto the end" (Matthew 24:13) clarifies that we are concerned with the entire duration of the Great Tribulation (another reason the Church of Jesus Christ cannot be meant in this context: the Church will not have to endure the Great Tribulation because it will have been raptured).

We established that Jesus was speaking to the Jews. A logical question that follows is: What time period was He speaking to them about?

The time is when God publicly begins to deal with Israel again, to lead His covenant people to the "end of the world" (verse 3), the return of her Messiah and His kingdom. Often, biblical prophecies involve a two- or even three-fold fulfillment: an initial fulfilment, a partial fulfillment and a main fulfillment (for instance, the first and second comings of Jesus, Pentecost, etc.).

Jesus' words in Matthew 24 focus on the last seven years of the 70th week of years mentioned in Daniel 9:24-27. The Lord was not talking about the course of the events, but of the "end of the world" (Matthew 24:3). The sign of the end of the age is the last, (i.e., the 70th week of years referred to by Daniel, the Great Tribulation, the "time of Jacob's trouble"— Jeremiah 30:7).

The Division of the Last Seven Years (Matthew 24)

All the signs the Lord Jesus mentioned in Matthew 24, which will ultimately lead to His visible return (Matthew 24:30), have a parallel in Revelation 6-19. The Church, remember, will be raptured at that time "from the hour of temptation" (Revelation 3:10).

The parallels between the events described in Matthew 24 and the seals in Revelation 6 are as follows:

•Matthew 24:4-5 – deception = first seal (Revelation 6:1-2).

•Matthew 24:6-7 – wars = second seal (Revelation 6:3-4).

•Matthew 24:7 – famine = third seal (Revelation 6:5-6).

• Matthew 24:7 – plagues = fourth seal (Revelation 6:7-8).

• Matthew 24:9-11 – persecution = fifth seal (Revelation 6:9-11).

• Matthew 24:12 – anarchy and the undermining of all existing ordinances = sixth seal (Revelation 6:12-17).

• Matthew 24:15-27 – Great Tribulation = seventh seal (as a bridge from Revelation 6:17 to 8:1ff).

This provides us with the following picture:

1. The first half of the Tribulation is described in Matthew 24:4-14 (the first six seals of Revelation 6).

2. The Great Tribulation is explained in Matthew 24:15-28 (the seven trumpets of judgment from Revelation 8:2ff and the seven bowls of wrath from Revelation 16:1ff).

3. The end of the Tribulation and the return of Jesus are described in Matthew 24:29-33 (Revelation 19).

The middle of the 70th week of years is referred to in Matthew 24:15ff, where the division of the seven-year Tribulation occurs. The abomination of desolation was only partly fulfilled in 70 A.D. with the destruction of the temple, for it refers to the statement in the book of Daniel, which clearly points to the end-times (Daniel 12:1,4,7,9,11).

The abomination of desolation was *prefulfilled* in 150 B.C. by Antiochus Epiphanes, which is mentioned in Daniel 11:31. Antiochus forbade the Jewish sacrifices in the temple, but set up an altar to

Zeus and sacrificed a pig to him upon it. Then the abomination of desolation was *partially fulfilled* in 70 A.D. when the Romans destroyed the temple. The abomination of desolation the Lord Jesus referred to in Matthew 24:15 will be *fulfilled* by the Antichrist in the middle of the last seven years before the return of Christ (Daniel 12). This speaks clearly about the time of the end (verses 4, 9), of a tribulation such as there has never been before (verse 1) and of "a time, times, and an half" (verse 7). This can be compared with Revelation 13:1, where the first beast comes from out of the sea and the second beast from out of the earth (verse 11), and with 2 Thessalonians 2:4 where "the man of sin," "the son of perdition...sitteth in the temple of God, shewing himself that he is God." The Lord Jesus spoke about the Great Tribulation in Matthew 24:21 (compare Jeremiah 30:7 and Revelation 16:18). In verses 16-28 the Lord Jesus explained what the remnant of the Jews should do at that time:

- They are to flee (verse 16; compare with Revelation 12:6).
- The days will be shortened to three-and-a-half years so that the elect will be saved (verse 22).
- They are to beware of false christs and prophets, for in a time of crisis many rumors will be spread that the Messiah is staying in a secret place (verses 23-24).
- False christs and prophets will perform signs and wonders (verse 24; compare with Revelation 13:13-14).
- But then the Lord will come at last "as the light-

ning cometh out of the east, and shineth even unto the west" (verse 27), and He will save them.

•These days of God's revenge (Luke 21:22), (i.e. the wrath of God and the Lamb - Revelation 6:16-17), are described in Matthew 24:28: "Wheresoever the carcase is, there will the eagles be gathered together." The carcass represents apostate Judaism and the world system under the rule of the Antichrist where death and Hades rule. The eagles represent the judgment of God. When the Lord used the Chaldeans to judge His idolatrous people, the prophet wrote: "their horsemen shall come from far; they shall fly as the eagle that hasteth to eat" (Habakkuk 1:8)

I don't believe the Lord Jesus was speaking about the 70 A.D. destruction of the temple in Matthew 24, but about the endtimes. Luke wrote about the destruction of the temple and of Jerusalem, and then he built a bridge to the endtimes (Chapter 21). That is the blessing of having the four Gospels, each of which shows us events from a different angle. It is not without reason that prophecy is divided in the Gospel accounts, for we should also divide the Scriptures correctly (2 Timothy 2:15).

Luke recorded something Matthew left out: "And when ye shall see Jerusalem compassed with armies, then know that the desolation thereof is nigh...And they shall fall by the edge of the sword, and shall be led away captive into all nations; and Jerusalem shall be trodden down of the Gentiles, until the times of the Gentiles be fulfilled" (Luke 21:20, 24). This desolation and dispersion of the Jews was fulfilled in 70 A.D. On the other hand, Matthew 24 includes the abomination of desolation (verse 15), which was not mentioned in Luke's account because it will only be fulfilled during the endtimes.

In Luke's account of the destruction of the temple in 70 A.D., we read that there will be "great distress" on earth (Greek—*anagke megale*) (Luke 21:23), not "great tribulation" (Greek—*thlipsis megaile*): "such as was not since the beginning of the world to this time, no, nor ever shall be" (Mathew 24:21). The "great distress" of 70 A.D. is clearly different from the Great Tribulation of the last times.

The Lesson for Us Today

The events of the coming Great Tribulation are casting a shadow, and the Rapture of the Church of Jesus Christ must be closer than ever. Many signs Jesus said would point to the end of the age are visible even now. For example:

•**Wars and rumors of wars:** The majority of the world's population has become restless. Many nations are engaged in war, and it is becoming clear that devastating wars will be possible in the near future. Almost a half a million scientists are concerned with improving existing weapons systems or working on inventing new ones.

•**"Fearful sights" (Luke 21:11):** These frightening

occurrences point to the increasing terror in our day.

• **World hunger:** The vast majority of the world's population is hungry. In fact, as much as 60 percent of the people in Africa have less to eat than what the United Nations Organization considers the daily minimum necessary for survival.

• **Earthquakes, storms, floods, other natural catastrophes and incurable diseases:** All these phenomena are increasing dramatically.

• **Persecutions:** A large majority of Christians is being persecuted; many even speak of an ever-decreasing spiral and of a culmination of persecution in recent years.

• **Oppression of Israel:** That tiny nation is becoming more and more oppressed, and Jerusalem in particular has become an explosive topic.

• **Deception abounds:** False religions are gaining an upper hand. The cry for a "strong man" is becoming louder. All sorts of things are being offered as "God" or "Savior," and people are grasping at them longingly. At the same time, apostasy from the Bible and the living God is increasing.

Mankind is being led to a point where he will eventually feel like there is no way out. But then the heavens will open and Jesus Christ will return. The birth pangs of the Great Tribulation will herald the coming of the Son of Man. A pregnant woman does not ponder the end of her life, but the beginning of a new life. We aren't standing on the threshold of the end of the world, but of the end of our age

(Matthew 24:3). The Son of God will not bring us to the end, but to a new beginning.

Jesus Christ is the hope of the future for each person who calls upon His name. But those who do not want Him will, like Israel, find that their hearts have become empty and desolate, while those who have received Him (John 1:12) will be filled with His presence. The Lord will come and dwell with such born-again people, who will find refuge, peace and protection under the shadow of His wings (Psalm 91:1-4).

The One who spoke the words of judgment over Jerusalem and the temple, "there shall not be left here one stone upon another, that shall not be thrown down" (Matthew 24:2), says this about Israel's future, which is connected with the future of the nations: "For thus saith the LORD of hosts; Yet once, it is a little while, and I will shake the heavens, and the earth, and the sea, and the dry land; and I will shake all nations, and the desire of all nations shall come: and I will fill this house with glory, saith the LORD of hosts. The silver is mine, and the gold is mine, saith the LORD of hosts. The glory of this latter house shall be greater than of the former, saith the LORD of hosts: and in this place will I give peace, saith the LORD of hosts" (Haggai 2:6-9).

The Jews will cry out when their Messiah, the Lord Jesus Christ, returns at the end of the Great Tribulation in great power and glory: "Blessed is he that cometh in the name of the LORD: God is the

LORD, which hath shewed us light" (Psalm 118:26-27).

1. *Nachrichten aus Israel* (German edition of *News from Israel*) 05/94

Chapter 2

THE GREAT LIBERATION

Imagine yourself in a brightly lit room full of activity and chaos. Suddenly the lights go out and an atmosphere of panic develops. But then a light appears in one corner, and nothing but this light can be seen. Everyone looks toward this light in expectation of what is about to happen. That is how it will be when Jesus returns to the earth.

" Immediately after the tribulation of those days shall the sun be darkened, and the moon shall not give her light, and the stars shall fall from heaven, and the powers of the heavens shall be shaken: and then shall appear the sign of the Son of man in heaven: and then shall all the tribes of the earth mourn, and they shall see the Son of man coming in the clouds of heaven with power and great glory" (Matthew 24:29-31).

These verses refer to the day of great liberation after the seven-year Great Tribulation has come to a close and the Lord Jesus returns to the earth. At that time, the eyes of the world will be focused on Israel.

The Climax of the Great Tribulation

The nations will be led to a point where they will feel like there is no way out. But at that moment the heavens will open up and Jesus Christ will return to the earth.

The birth pangs of the Great Tribulation will herald the coming of the Son of Man. It will be similar to a pregnant woman whose contractions have reached the point where she can hardly bear them, and then suddenly she delivers a new life. The climax of the Great Tribulation will bring back the Son of God, and with it new life. That is why we do not speak about the end of the world. Jesus will bring great liberation and a completely new beginning to Israel and this world. Jesus is the hope of the future. He is the hope of every soul who calls upon His name. Every person, even those who are in deep distress, may know that he or she can come to Jesus and He will bring light to the darkest corner of his or her soul. Jesus can make new what appears to be lost. He said, "I am come a light into the world, that whosoever believeth on me should not abide in darkness" (John 12:46).

The climax of the Great Tribulation is described in Matthew 24:29: "Immediately after the tribulation of those days shall the sun be darkened, and the moon shall not give her light, and the stars shall fall from heaven, and the powers of the heavens shall be shaken."

Jesus described it as being a terrible time, "such as was not since the beginning of the world to this time, no, nor ever shall be" (verse 21). There is no increase of intensity in the Great Tribulation. The Lord described it as a time like a dead, decayed carcass, upon which the eagles are already feeding (compare verse 28). One would think that all hope would be gone and no further life would be possible.

Great events cast their shadow far ahead of them. The signs are a part of the last seven years before Jesus returns. We are experiencing in an increasing measure the stronger signs of the worst that is still to come. It is as though our world is slowly but surely approaching a catastrophic climax. The following quotations confirm this:

> • "In my opinion, we can rightly suppose that God is setting the scene for His tremendous endtime program." [1]

- "There are more fulfilled signs than in any previous era." [2]
- "I would like to point out that within the last decade strange phenomena have occurred in the realm of nature. Terrible natural catastrophes have increased in number and intensity." [3]
- "On the present-day world stage many things lead to the conclusion that the end of this age is imminent...never before in world history has there been such a coincidence of important signs of the preparation of the end." [4]
- "In our present time preparatory developments are casting their shadow ahead of them...apostasy in the religious field... preparation for a restoration of the Roman Empire...the return of Israel...strengthening of the previous enemies of Israel... These developments are setting the stage for the events of the time of Tribulation." [5]

According to the words of the Lord Jesus, the Great Tribulation will come to an end in that the sun will be darkened. Since the moon is lit by the sun, it will likewise cease to provide light. The power of the heavens will be shaken and even the stars will fall from the sky (compare with Isaiah 13:10 and Revelation 6:12-13). God has supernaturally intervened in history. For instance, when the Old Covenant was introduced on Mount Sinai (Exodus 19:16ff) during Joshua's time, "the sun stood still, and the moon stayed" (Joshua 10:13); and during the time of Hezekiah, God said, "Behold, I will bring again the shadow of the degrees, which is gone down in the sun dial of Ahaz, ten degrees backward. So the sun returned ten degrees, by which degrees it was gone down" (Isaiah 38:8).

The prophet Joel wrote (and the Apostle Peter refers to this in his speech at Pentecost), "And I will shew wonders in the heavens and in the earth, blood, and fire, and pillars of smoke [volcanoes]. The sun shall be turned into darkness, and the moon into blood, before the great and the terrible day of the LORD come" (Joel 2:30-31, compare also to Acts 2:20).

I believe the heavenly bodies really will be darkened for two reasons:

1. The attack of Jerusalem by hostile nations will come to an end. Satan and his demons will gather all the nations against Israel through the Antichrist at Armageddon (Revelation 16:13-16). They will pounce like eagles on a carcass (Matthew 24:28). The Lord also spoke of this through the prophet Joel: "For behold in those days, and in that time, when I shall bring again the captivity of Judah and Jerusalem, I will also gather all nations, and will bring them down into the valley of Jehoshaphat, and will plead with them there for my people and for my heritage Israel, whom they have scattered among the nations, and parted my land…Multitudes, multitudes in the valley of decision: for the day of the LORD is near in the valley of decision. The sun and the moon shall be darkened, and the stars shall withdraw their

shining. The LORD also shall roar out of Zion, and utter his voice from Jerusalem; and the heavens and the earth shall shake: but the LORD will be the hope of his people, and the strength of the children of Israel" (Joel 3:1-2, 14-17). No one will be able to fight, and airplanes will not be able to fly when "the heavens and the earth shall shake" and darkness reigns.

2. The heavenly bodies will be darkened so that nothing can prevent mankind from seeing Jesus illuminated in all His glory. Revelation 1:7 is worded so majestically: "Behold, he cometh with clouds; and every eye shall see him."

God will supernaturally intervene and allow unprecedented natural phenomena to occur. Bible scholar William MacDonald wrote:

> "A description of the events that would take place if a heavenly body were to hit the earth and the earth's axis were displaced may give us a feeble idea of what this will be like. An earthquake would shake the earth; air and water would continue to move through inertia. Hurricanes would rage over land and sea; the sea would flood the continents and carry with it sand, stones and sea creatures. Friction heat would arise everywhere melting rocks, volcanoes would break out, lava would come out of cracks in the earth's crust and cover great territories. Mountains would arise in plains and cover other mountains, thereby creating faults and chasms in the earth. Lakes would be

shaken and emptied, rivers seek new beds; great land areas would sink into the sea with all their inhabitants. Forests would burn; storms and sea masses would tear them out of the ground they are growing on and pile them up with branches and roots to make high mountains. Lakes would become deserts because their water flows from them." [6]

The Creator of heaven and earth can so shake the world that everything would be upside-down, but He can also keep it so that its inhabitants survive.

The Return of the Lord

Matthew 24:30 describes the Second Coming: "And then shall appear the sign of the Son of man in heaven: and then shall all the tribes of the earth mourn, and they shall see the Son of man coming in the clouds of heaven with power and great glory." The distress that comes from the Great Tribulation will bring the Lord Jesus back for judgment, but also for great liberation. The return of Christ will be the most dramatic event since the Fall of man in the Garden of Eden, and it will be the climax of God's plan.

Verse 30 can be divided into three segments, which is not coincidental:

1. "Then shall appear the sign of the Son of man in heaven."

The phrase "Son of man" is a typical description that is understood in Israel. Daniel saw Him in spirit and described Him (Daniel 7:13-14). The "sign of the Son of man" is the visible sign of His glory (perhaps the Shekinah; that is, the pillar of cloud or fire of the glory of the God of Israel, an all-surpassing light).

Recorded in the book of Ezekiel is a prophetic portrayal of how the Lord's glory left the temple on account of Israel's sins (Ezekiel 11:2-3), and then ascended from the middle of Jerusalem to the Mount of Olives: "Now the cherubims stood on the right side of the house, when the man went in; and the cloud filled the inner court. Then the glory of the LORD went up from the cherub, and stood over the threshold of the house; and the house was filled with the cloud, and the court was full of the brightness of the LORD's glory" (Ezekiel 10:3-4). "Then did the cherubims lift up their wings, and the wheels beside them; and the glory of the God of Israel was over them above. And the glory of the LORD went up from the midst of the city, and stood upon the mountain which is on the east side of the city" (Ezekiel 11:22-23).

Ezekiel 43 contains the description of how the glory of God returned for Israel's restoration; it came from the East (the Mount of Olives), and it will fill the temple of the millennium of peace. Among other things, we read: "Afterward he brought me to the gate, even the gate that looketh toward the east: and, behold, the glory of the God of Israel came from the way of the east: and his voice was like a noise of many waters: and the earth shined with his glory...So the spirit took me up, and brought me into the inner court; and, behold, the glory of the LORD filled the house...And he said unto me, Son of man, the place of my throne, and the place of the soles of my feet, where I will dwell in the midst of the children of Israel for ever, and my holy name, shall the house of Israel no more defile, neither they, nor their kings, by their whoredom, nor by the carcases of their kings in their high places" (verses 1-2, 5, 7).

When the Lord Jesus finished His judgment upon Israel and Jerusalem (Matthew 23:37-39), we read: "And Jesus went out, and departed from the temple" (Matthew 24:1). Then He went to the Mount of Olives (verse 3), and after His resurrection He ascended from there into heaven (Acts 1:9). He did what the prophet Ezekiel had already described.

Jesus delivered His endtime speech about Israel's welfare during the Great Tribulation, Daniel's 70th week of years. He will return in glory at the end of this time in the manner in which we have just read in Ezekiel, "and the earth shined with his glory." In this connection, Zechariah wrote: "And the LORD my God shall come, and all the saints with thee (compare with Daniel 7:10; Jude 14 and Revelation 5:11). "And it shall come to pass in that day, that the light shall not be clear, nor dark: But it shall be one day which shall be known to the LORD, not day, nor night: but it shall come to pass, that at evening time it shall be light" (Zechariah 14:6-7). Jesus Christ will come as the "Sun of righteousness" (Malachi 4:2, compare also with Psalm 50:1-6; 45:1-17 and 18:10-21).

2. "Then shall all the tribes of the earth mourn."

The "sign of the Son of man"—that is, His glory—will appear in heaven before the Lord Himself appears because the Jews will recognize their God by this sign. Certainly the eternal God does not need to do this, but here a new connection to the Old Covenant is made. This glory is a well-known term for the Jewish people (think about the Exodus from Egypt, 40 years of wandering in the desert, the prophecies of the prophet Ezekiel and the Psalms.) They will become prepared through this for the Son of God to appear and to enable them to receive Him with due honor. For this reason, we read, "and then shall all the tribes of the earth mourn." They will see His glory and recognize that He is their God, who had already been with them under the Old Covenant. That's when they will repent. Then Zechariah's prophecy will be fulfilled, "And I will pour upon the house of David, and upon the inhabitants of Jerusalem, the spirit of grace and of supplications: and they shall look upon me whom they have pierced, and they shall mourn for him, as one mourneth for his only son, and shall be in bitterness for him, as one that is in bitterness for his firstborn" (Zechariah 12:10). Then every man, woman and child will repent (compare verses 11-14). This weeping in repentance will ultimately turn into rejoicing:

"For his anger endureth but a moment; in his favour is life; weeping may endure for a night, but joy cometh in the morning" (Psalm 30:5).

3. **"And they shall see the Son of man coming in the clouds of heaven with power and great glory."**

Then the Jews will be able to receive the Lord Jesus as their Messiah, and what He had prophesied will be fulfilled, "Ye shall not see me henceforth, till ye shall say, Blessed is he that cometh in the name of the Lord" (Matthew 23:39). Yes, then the time will come when they see "the Son of man coming in the clouds of heaven with power and great glory."

The Consequences of Jesus' Return

We read in Matthew 24:31: "And he shall send his angels with a great sound of a trumpet, and they shall gather together his elect from the four winds, from one end of heaven to the other." Since we can mention only a few of the many events that will take place, we will focus on Jerusalem.

• Isaiah 11:12 explains that the Lord Jesus will bring home all believing Jews who will have been dispersed by persecution and tribulation: "And he shall set up an ensign for the nations, and shall assemble the outcasts of Israel, and gather together the dispersed of Judah from the four corners of the earth" (compare with Isaiah 66:20 and Ezekiel 37:21-22).

• Judgment will take place upon the Jewish survivors of the Tribulation (Ezekiel 20:34-38). This judgment is also the object of Jesus' speech in

Matthew 25:1-30.

• Then Israel will find its way to the One it had not wanted: "O Jerusalem, Jerusalem, thou that killest the prophets, and stonest them which are sent unto thee, how often would I have gathered thy children together, even as a hen gathereth her chickens under her wings, and ye would not!" (Matthew 23:37).

"But unto you that fear my name shall the Sun of righteousness arise with healing in his wings; and ye shall go forth, and grow up as calves of the stall" (Malachi 4:2).

Israel will receive the Spirit of God; the tribes of Judah and Israel will be joined together (Ezekiel 37:16-22). The entire land will be forgiven of everything in one day (Zechariah 3:9). And the Lord Jesus will reign as king in Israel's midst (compare Psalm 46:5-6, 9-11).

• All the nations will be amazed and terrified that a people they so hated will be the people of the one living God. The Lord used the prophet Jeremiah to write: "And it shall be to me a name of joy, a praise and an honour before all the nations of the earth, which shall hear all the good that I do unto them; and they shall fear and tremble for all the goodness and for all the prosperity that I procure unto it" (Jeremiah 33:9).

• Many other Gentile nations will join the people of God: "And many nations shall be joined to the LORD in that day, and shall be my people: and I will dwell in the midst of thee, and thou shalt know that the LORD of hosts hath sent me unto thee" (Zechariah 2:11, compare also with Psalm 47:8-9 & Ezekiel 47:21-23).

What Does the Imminent Return of Jesus Mean for Us Personally?

In the 19th century, a man in London wanted to hear two famous preachers one Sunday. He listened to one in the morning and when he came out of the church, he said to himself, "What a great preacher! I was so impressed by him!" In the afternoon, he went to another church, where well-known preacher Charles Haddon Spurgeon was preaching. When he left the church an hour later, he said, "What a wonderful Savior! What a mighty Lord we have!" That is how it will be when Jesus comes. All fame will be forgotten, and all human achievements will become insignificant; Jesus will amaze everyone. He will establish the kingdom that mankind has desired for thousands of years. Jesus will bring with Him peace and righteousness.

My dear friends, where will you be then? Acts 17:30-31 explains: "And the times of this ignorance God winked at; but now commandeth all men every where to repent: because he hath appointed a day, in the which he will judge the world in righteousness by that man whom he hath ordained; whereof he hath given assurance unto all men, in that he hath raised him from the dead."

Those who have come to Christ are safe forever.

The Lord is seeking people today to whom He can impart His grace.

1 - 5 are taken from the book, *When the Trumpet Sounds* by Thomas Ice and Timothy Demy, Copyright 1995, Harvest House Publishers.

6. *Commentary of the New Testament*, Volume 1 by William McDonald

Chapter 3

THE FIG TREE

The Jewish generation that "sees all these things"—that is, the one that sees the signs of the Great Tribulation and goes through them—will be the same generation that witnesses the return of Jesus. In this chapter we will carefully consider the events outlined in the parable of the fig tree.

"" Now learn a parable of the fig tree; When his branch is yet tender, and putteth forth leaves, ye know that summer is nigh: so likewise ye, when ye shall see all these things, know that it is near, even at the doors. Verily I say unto you, This generation shall not pass, till all these things be fulfilled. Heaven and earth shall pass away, but my words shall not pass away" (Matthew 24:32-35).

Israel at Jesus' First Advent

The Lord Jesus continually blessed people while He was on earth: He forgave sins, healed the sick, raised the dead and performed many other miracles. Shortly before His death, however, He performed a "miracle of judgment": "Now in the morning as he returned into the city, he hungered. And when he saw a fig tree in the way, he came to it, and found nothing thereon, but leaves only, and said unto it, Let no fruit grow on thee henceforward for ever. And presently the fig tree withered away. And when the disciples saw it, they marvelled, saying, How soon is the fig tree withered away!" (Matthew 21:18-20).

Why did the Creator of heaven and earth curse this fig tree? It was a prophetic act that referred to the Jewish generation of that time that had rejected Him. German Bible translator Ludwig Albrecht commented:

> Every fig tree bearing leaves must have unripe figs in the first half of April, which are very popular in Palestine. The fig tree was deceptive and

hypocritical in this way, so it was a fitting picture
of Jerusalem and her temple. There also the Lord
found no fruit, although with regard to the outward formalities of the law a promising show of
leaves were visible from afar.

The context surrounding the account of the fig tree
in Matthew 21 includes a description of the cleansing
of the temple, an account of the annoyance of the
high priests, the critical question concerning Jesus'
authority, the parable of the two sons, and the parable of the vineyard workers. All of this content points
in the same direction.

Every sentence Jesus spoke illustrated a historical
and spiritual truth. The situation directly preceding
Jesus' cursing of the fig tree was the cleansing of the
temple, which annoyed the Pharisees. Then Matthew
21:17 states: "And he left them, and went out of the
city into Bethany; and he lodged there." This took
place before the Lord saw the fig tree on the following day. So this is a hint that Jesus was about to leave
His nation, which had been spiritually barren. He left
and traveled to Bethany, where lived the few people
in Israel who still loved Him (Lazarus, Mary and
Martha). Is it a coincidence that the word "Bethany"
means "house of figs"? It is as if the Lord was hint-
ing at what He was seeking: fruit. He left those who
were barren in order to stay with those who produced
fruit.

On the following morning, He left Bethany and
traveled in the direction of Jerusalem, and that which

followed reflects Israel's situation at that time.

On the following morning...

"...when he saw a fig tree in the way, he came to it." Jesus came to His people for the first time then, and offered Himself to them as their Messiah. He entered Jerusalem on a donkey and let the people pay homage to Him as their king.

"...he hungered..." Jesus hungered to bless the people at His First Advent, but He also sought fruit of the seed that His Father had sown over the centuries through the mouths of the prophets. But the Jewish generation of that time had leaves (outward piety); they had the Word of God, but they had no fruit—true faith in Jesus Christ.

The Lord Jesus ministered in Israel and Jerusalem for three years. He was about 30 years old (compare Luke 3:23) when He began His public ministry and He probably died at the age of 33. He performed signs and wonders, and introduced Himself to His people as the Messiah of God. He worked on His people, but the majority of them did not want to believe in Him. The Lord made this clear in another parable, "A certain man had a fig tree planted in his vineyard; and he came and sought fruit thereon, and found none. Then said he unto the dresser of his vineyard, Behold, these three years I come seeking fruit on this fig tree [For three years Jesus came to the Passover feast in Jerusalem and worked there], and find none: cut it down; why encumbereth it the ground? And he answering said unto him, Lord, let it alone this year also, till I shall dig about it, and dung it: and if it bear fruit, well: and if not, then after that thou shalt cut it down" (Luke 13:6-9).

In the parable, Israel is the vineyard and Jerusalem is the fig tree in the midst of the vineyard. God the Father is the owner of the vineyard, and God the Son is the dresser of the vineyard (compare Isaiah 3:14 & 5:7; Jeremiah 24:5, 8). The Lord tended the fig tree for three years, but it bore no fruit. What Jesus taught about it had to be fulfilled: "If not, then after that thou shalt cut it down." The generation of that time was rejected. It literally withered, was cut down and never bore fruit again. A few days later Israel also rejected her King, which Jesus had prophesied before in the parable of the ten pounds: "We will not have this man to reign over us" (Luke 19:14).

It was not long (70 A.D.) before the Romans came and destroyed Jerusalem. The land ceased to exist politically, and the Jews were dispersed all over the world. Jesus' words and parables concerning the generation of that time were literally fulfilled. Then the prophet Joel's prophecy from centuries before was also fulfilled: "The vine is dried up, and the fig tree languisheth; the pomegranate tree, the palm tree also, and the apple tree, even all the trees of the field, are withered: because joy is withered away from the sons of men" (Joel 1:12). The whole land withered because Israel and Jerusalem withered.

The Jewish land had become a valley of weeping. From that time on, the Jews in the Diaspora wept

45

over the loss of their land, Jerusalem, and their temple. For almost 2,000 years they called to one another, "Next year in Jerusalem!"

We must take God very seriously. He is also coming to you and calling you to Himself through His Son Jesus Christ, who did everything for you and for me on Calvary's cross. It is extremely dangerous to postpone your decision to follow Christ (compare with Job 33:29-30).

There are by no means few who attend church each Sunday, who listen to the Word of God, who sing in the church choir or participate in prayer meetings, and yet still are not converted. I also know church elders and pastors who bear the responsibility for their churches, but who are not themselves converted.

Blessed are all those who have accepted the Lord Jesus Christ and His accomplished work for themselves personally! What about you? Have you already taken this most important step in your life? If not, I am calling upon you to do it today because Jesus has been working on you for a long time.

Israel Before the Return of Jesus

In the parable of the fig tree, Jesus said that the tree should be cut down. The disciples witnessed Jesus' curse of the barren fig tree and its subsequent withering.

Regarding His return, the Lord said, "Now learn a parable of the fig tree; when his branch is yet tender, and putteth forth leaves, ye know that summer is nigh: so likewise ye, when ye shall see all these things, know that it is near, even at the doors. Verily I say unto you, This generation shall not pass, till all these things be fulfilled" (Matthew 24:32-34). When the Lord told this parable of the reawakening fig tree, the disciples were still affected by the withered fig tree. How it must have surprised them that Jesus suddenly spoke again about the fig tree, of a new generation and of His return!

When the disciples saw the withered fig tree that the Lord had cursed, we read, "And when the disciples saw it, they marvelled, saying, How soon is the fig tree withered away! Jesus answered and said unto them, Verily I say unto you, If ye have faith, and doubt not, ye shall not only do this which is done to the fig tree, but also if ye shall say unto this mountain, Be thou removed, and be thou cast into the sea; it shall be done" (Matthew 21:20-21).

It seems that the Lord Jesus wanted to proclaim then what would one day come to pass. He taught His disciples how important it is to believe instead of doubt, as the generation of that time had done. He told them that if faith made it possible to cause a fig tree to wither or cast a mountain into the sea (Luke 17:6), then that which is humanly impossible would take place, and the fig tree would blossom again and bear fruit. He didn't refer to the generation of that time, of course, but to a new Jewish generation.

Jesus said that great obstacles could be removed by faith. And sure enough, in the 20th century, the "mountains" of nationalism/socialism, Leninism, and Stalinism sank into the sea, but the kingdom of God grew through people who believed in God the Father, Jesus His Son, and the biblical promises of the Eternal God. The fig tree, the Jewish people, has also awakened to new life.

The generation of the time in which Jesus lived and worked sank, fruitless. But according to His words, a new generation would arise that would witness His return. This is the point Jesus wanted to make clear through His endtime parable of the fig tree.

The vineyard as such represents the Jewish state. Israel has existed as a nation since 1948. Here we are concerned with the national significance and restoration of the people and the land. In a deeper sense, the fig tree is an example of Jerusalem, which was planted as Israel's capital since 1967. The sap and the leaves of the fig tree symbolize the spiritual restoration of a new generation of the Jewish people. The fruit of the late figs is the fruit that will be ripe when Jesus Christ returns for His people. This fruit is the best in Israel. The "late" figs will be the believing remnant in Israel. They will go through the Tribulation and witness the return of Jesus.

Chapter 4

THE LAST EIGHT PEOPLE OF THE OLD WORLD

Only eight people survived the catastrophic Flood. This shocking fact shows that it is not the masses who are right, but only those who take the Word of God seriously.

" But of that day and hour knoweth no man, no, not the angels of heaven, but my Father only. But as the days of Noe were, so shall also the coming of the Son of man be. For as in the days that were before the flood they were eating and drinking, marrying and giving in marriage, until the day that Noe entered into the ark, and knew not until the flood came, and took them all away; so shall also the coming of the Son of man be. Then shall two be in the field; the one shall be taken, and the other left. Two women shall be grinding at the mill; the one shall be taken, and the other left. Watch therefore: for ye know not what hour your Lord doth come" (Matthew 24:36-42).

"For if God...spared not the old world, but saved Noah the eighth person, a preacher of righteousness, bringing in the flood upon the world of the ungodly" (2 Peter 2:4-5).

The Return of Jesus Christ for Israel

I believe it is incorrect to interpret Matthew 24:36-42, which refers to the days of Noah, as having anything to do with the Rapture of the Church. This is not about the Rapture, but is a continued description of the Great Tribulation, at the end of which Jesus will return as the Son of man to set up His kingdom.

The phrase "Son of man" is generally used in connection with the Jewish people, "And then shall appear the sign of the Son of man in heaven; and then shall all the tribes of the earth mourn, and they shall see the Son of man coming in the clouds of heaven with power and great glory" (Matthew 24:30). This refers to Jesus' return as the Son of man to redeem the Jewish people.

But about the time of Noah, we read, "As the days of Noe were, so shall also the coming of the Son of man be" (Matthew 24:37). Because this again is speaking of the Son of man, we are concerned with the same return that is mentioned in verse 30. Daniel also made this clear (the Church had not even been revealed in the Old Testament) when he wrote, "I saw in the night visions, and, behold, one like the Son of man came with the clouds of heaven, and came to the Ancient of days, and they brought him near before him. And there was given him dominion, and glory, and a kingdom, that all people, nations, and languages, should serve him: his dominion is an everlasting dominion, which shall not pass away, and his kingdom that which shall not be destroyed" (Daniel 7:13-14).

It is also apparent from Matthew 10:21-23 that His return as the Son of man is for Israel: "And the brother shall deliver up the brother to death, and the father the child: and the children shall rise up against their parents, and cause them to be put to death. And ye shall be hated of all men for my name's sake: but he that endureth to the end shall be saved. But when they persecute you in this city, flee ye into another: for verily I say unto you, Ye shall not have gone over the cities of Israel, till the Son of man be come" (compare also with Revelation 14:14). The return of the Son of man is always connected with Israel: "Ye shall not have gone over the cities of Israel, till the Son of man be come." Therefore, Matthew chapters 24 and 25 cannot possibly refer to the Rapture.

The Great Tribulation and the Last Chance for Salvation

The Jews who are being addressed in Jesus' Olivet Discourse will have to go through the Great Tribulation, for during this time it will be decided which of them will ultimately be able to enter the millennium of peace.

Immediately following the Rapture, in the first half of the last seven years, those Jews who have come to believe in Jesus will proclaim the Gospel of the kingdom and His imminent return.

The 144,000 Jews out of Israel will be chosen and sealed (Revelation 7:4ff), and the two witnesses will appear on the scene (Revelation 11:3ff). A Messianic remnant will be formed. These believing Jews will invite men to accept salvation in Jesus Christ in the face of threatening catastrophes, as did Noah, the preacher of righteousness. A majority of the people in Israel will then be converted and will receive the salvation of their Messiah. Some of the Jews, however, will hold fast to the covenant with the Antichrist. They will receive his number, "the number of a man" (Revelation 13:18). Many in Israel will be persecuted, will betray one another and will deliver one another (Matthew 10:21-23).

Peter was an apostle to the Jews, so both of his letters were addressed to them (1 Peter 1:1 and 2 Peter 3:1). To these he calls to remembrance, "Knowing this first, that there shall come in the last days scoffers, walking after their own lusts, and saying, Where is the promise of his coming? For since the fathers fell asleep, all things continue as they were from the beginning of the creation. For this they willingly are ignorant of, that by the word of God the heavens were of old, and the earth standing out of the water and in the water; whereby the world that then was, being overflowed with water, perished" (2 Peter 3:3-6). With the term "the fathers," Peter was obviously referring to the Jewish patriarchs who had prophetically looked for the Messiah and His kingdom.

This hope will again be proclaimed in Israel during the Great Tribulation, but many will merely shake their heads in mockery and disbelief. Then, however, the judgments of the second half of the Tribulation will come upon Israel and the rest of the world like a flood. For instance, the prophet Daniel wrote, "and the end thereof shall be with a flood, and unto the end of the war desolations are determined" (Daniel 9:26).

Judgment After Jesus Returns

Here the decision of who will and who will not enter the Millennial Kingdom will be made: "But as the days of Noe were, so shall also the coming of the

Son of man be. For as in the days that were before the flood they were eating and drinking, marrying and giving in marriage, until the day that Noe entered into the ark, and knew not until the flood came, and took them all away; so shall also the coming of the Son of man be. Then shall two be in the field; the one shall be taken, and the other left. Two women shall be grinding at the mill; the one shall be taken, and the other shall be left" (Matthew 24:37-41).

Not all will be taken away at the "flood" of the Great Tribulation as during Noah's time; there will be a division: "Then two shall be in the field; the one shall be taken [in judgment], and the other left," to enter into the Millennial Kingdom. "Two women shall be grinding at the mill; the one shall be taken [snatched away]; and the other left," to enter the kingdom. Luke the evangelist, adds, "In that night there shall be two men [i.e. people – NIV] in one bed [presumably a married couple]; the one shall be taken [snatched away], and the other shall be left" (Luke 17:34), also to enter into the Messianic kingdom.

Jesus' words are in complete agreement with the Old Testament, for the prophet Zephaniah had already spoken of this judgment in Zephaniah 3:11-13, "In that day shalt thou not be ashamed for all thy doings, wherein thou hast transgressed against me; for then I will take away out of the midst of thee them that rejoice in thy pride, and thou shalt no more be haughty because of my holy mountain. I will also leave in the midst of thee an afflicted and poor peo-

54

ple, and they shall trust in the name of the LORD. The remnant of Israel shall not do iniquity, nor speak lies; neither shall a deceitful tongue be found in their mouth: for they shall feed and lie down, and none shall make them afraid."

God spoke in the same way through the prophet Ezekiel: "Like as I pleaded with your fathers in the wilderness of the land of Egypt, so will I plead with you, saith the Lord GOD. And I will cause you to pass under the rod, and I will bring you into the bond of the covenant: and I will purge out from among you the rebels, and them that transgress against me: I will bring them forth out of the country where they sojourn, and they shall not enter into the land of Israel: and ye shall know that I am the LORD" (Ezekiel 20:36-38).

The prophet Malachi wrote: "Then they that feared the LORD spake often one to another: and the LORD hearkened, and heard it, and a book of remembrance was written before him for them that feared the LORD, and that thought upon his name. And they shall be mine, saith the LORD of hosts, in that day when I make up my jewels; and I will spare them, as a man spareth his own son that serveth him. Then shall ye return, and discern between the righteous and the wicked, between him that serveth God and him that serveth him not" (Malachi 3:16-20).

The Lord Jesus said, "For I am come to set a man at variance against his father, and the daughter against her mother, and the daughter-in-law against her mother-in-law. And a man's foes shall be they of his own household" (Matthew 10:35-36). Perhaps father and son will be working in the same field, and the judgment will divide them. Perhaps mother-in-law and daughter-in-law will be working at the same mill, and will then be separated from one another in judgment.

Application for Today

In spite of the fact that Jesus' endtime discourse upon the Mount of Olives primarily concerned Israel and the Great Tribulation, let us apply it to our time, for the coming events are casting their shadows ahead of them. It is not by chance that Noah's time is used as a warning example in the New Testament, particularly in the epistles.

It will be similar at the Rapture. The Lord will come suddenly and take His Church to heaven. This event will bring about an unprecedented, sudden and visible separation among the people of the nations in countries, cities and villages, in the streets and in their homes. People will suddenly become separated from all levels of society and from all circumstances. At that time it will become apparent who really belongs to Jesus and who does not.

The people will look the same on the outside, but the difference, which had always existed, will be in their hearts, and will become visible with ultimately tragic consequences. People will live together with their friends, families and neighbors for years. They will eat and speak with one another, travel and play games, and then suddenly everything will change. Because of such a radical difference in their hearts, some of them will go to be with Jesus in His heavenly kingdom, and the others will go to be judged.

They Lived in Godless Indifference

The Lord Jesus said, "For as in the days that were before the flood they were eating and drinking, marrying and giving in marriage, until the day that Noe entered into the ark, and knew not until the flood came, and took them all away; so shall also the coming of the Son of man be" (Matthew 24:38-39).

The people of that time had only one desire: To satisfy their own needs. Everything revolved around the here and now. They did not consider the Word of God, that its promises are being fulfilled, and that life on this earth is not everything.

Jesus did not mention the terrible sins that were being committed during Noah's time, although they were numerous (compare Genesis 6:1ff), but what was much worse than any sin was the indifference people had towards God. People did not include God in their lives. They lived without Him, in spite of the fact that the Spirit of God was working in their hearts: "My spirit shall not always strive with man" (Genesis 6:3). The worst of all sins is to arrange one's life without considering that there is a God. He is the God from whom all things come and for whom everything was made. The Lord speaks in love, mercy and with great sincerity, but people do not want to listen to Him: "And [they] knew not."

The Lord Jesus prayed, "This is life eternal, that they might know thee the only true God, and Jesus Christ, whom thou hast sent" (John 17:3). To know God is to live. Not to know Him is death. We should saturate ourselves with the things that pertain to eternal life. We can lose a lot on this earth, but there is more than that to be lost: eternal life now, and eternal glory at Jesus' return.

The important role food plays in society has reached a climax in our time, which the Lord warningly prophesied to happen in the endtimes, "Take heed to yourselves, lest at any time your hearts be overcharged with surfeiting, and drunkenness, and cares of this life, and so that day come upon you unawares. For as a snare shall it come on all them that dwell on the face of the whole earth. Watch ye therefore, and pray always, that ye may be accounted worthy to escape all these things that shall come to pass, and to stand before the Son of man" (Luke 21:34-36).

On the other hand, Noah cared about trusting God. Hebrews 11:7 says of him, "By faith Noah, being warned of God of things not seen as yet, moved with fear, prepared an ark to the saving of his house; by the which he condemned the world, and became heir of the righteousness which is by faith." This man wanted to survive, together with his whole family. He took the things God said seriously and put them into practice. We should be consumed with concern of being able to stand one day before the Son of man.

They Did Not Believe the Gospel of Jesus Christ

"For Christ also hath once suffered for sins, the just for the unjust, that he might bring us to God, being put to death in the flesh, but quickened by the Spirit; by which also he went and preached unto the spirits in prison; which sometime were disobedient, when once the longsuffering of God waited in the days of Noah, while the ark was a preparing, wherein few, that is, eight souls were saved by water" (1 Peter 3:18-20). The Holy Spirit of Jesus was already active in Noah, and he preached to the people of his generation as a "preacher of righteousness" (2 Peter 2:5). Ultimately the people didn't only disregard Noah, but they were rebelling against God. They remained stiff-necked to what they heard, and this sent them to their damnation.

Noah's generation is also referred to as the "world of the godless," for the people then strove with the Spirit of God. And so only eight people remained of the entire world population.

It is possible to mathematically calculate the world's population of that time. If we begin with six billion people today, factor in the losses of lives in wars and catastrophes, and do the math for roughly the last 4,500 years, we arrive at eight people. This is the time of Noah. If we begin with eight people and calculate 4,500 years forward, we arrive at six billion people alive at the beginning of the 21st century.

Had evolution been true, and man had existed for many millions of years, the world's population would now be unimaginably great.

Conclusive evidence of a flood in which only a few people survived can be found in a vast number of credible sources. Some scientists believe the Black Sea is the result of a great flood that came from the Bosporus and filled the gigantic valley. Houses have even been found at the bottom of the sea, strongly suggesting that people lived there before the flood.

Only Eight People Survived

Why did only eight people survive the Great Flood? The survivors are mentioned six times in the Bible (Genesis 6:18; 7:7,13; 8:18; 2 Peter 3:20 and 2 Peter 2:5).

• **Only those who survived entered the ark.**

Godless people lived at that time. These people had only lived for their passions and sins. They were mockers who denied the existence of God. But there were others: the elderly, children, young people, humanists, ideologists, pacifists and religious people. Perhaps some had been kindly disposed towards Noah. He probably had relatives. Surely some people felt sorry for him. He probably got along with some people and didn't get along with others. Some people may have even helped Noah. There may have been supporters who stood up for him before those who mocked him. It is striking that the people of that time did not try to hinder the building of the ark; they let him proceed with the construction. Yet they all perished. They had been close to the ark, but they did not enter it. It does not matter whether we are favorably disposed to Christianity. Nor does our social behavior, our friendship, our family relationships or our contribution to the work make a difference. Only entering the ark is what counts. The ark had only one door. This is a picture of Jesus Christ, who said, "I am the door: by me if any man enter in, he shall be saved" (John 10:9). The example of the ark is an example of the most serious and most holy and radical consequence. Only eight people were in the ark and were saved. Only Jesus Christ saves! God commanded the ark be covered with pitch so that no water could enter it. The Hebrew word for this comes from the root *kapar,* which means "to cover." Later on the sins of the Jews were covered with the sacrificial blood of lambs and goats, which is a picture of forgiveness through the blood of Jesus. The fatal flood of judgment will not destroy you if you are in Christ. Isn't this a great promise? "If any man be in Christ, he is a new creature" (2 Corinthians 5:17).

• **Because only eight people were saved at that time, we can see that from God's perspective numbers don't count.** During Noah's time only eight people were in the right and the rest of the world was in the wrong. Noah was wrong in the eyes of the world, but to God he was right because he trusted His Word. The Church of Jesus Christ is in the wrong in the eyes of this world, for instance, with its teaching about the Rapture (1 Thessalonians 4:16-18 and 1 Corinthians 15:51-53). People laughed at Noah for building his ark. The doctrine of the Rapture sounds so ridiculous to the world that quite a few Christians are too intimidated to speak about it. It is no different with the blood of Jesus Christ, forgiveness, heaven, and the return of Jesus Christ. It is not the masses that are right, nor is it the teachers, philosophers, scientists or politicians.

• **Only One is in the right: God!** Jesus Christ said, "I am...the truth" (John 14:6). Only those who are on His side will be right in the end, because God will say they are right.

Perhaps you are very near to having a relationship with God, but you are not yet safely inside of that relationship. Will you come in today? Jesus is saying to you personally, "I am the door: by me if any man enter in, he shall be saved"! (John 10:9).

Chapter 5

THE RETURN OF JESUS AND THE TIME OF LOT

The tragic fate of Sodom and Gomorrah is not just a story from the past, but a serious warning for the future. Do we dare to take these words from the mouth of the Lord Jesus and His apostle seriously today?

" Likewise also as it was in the days of Lot; they did eat, they drank, they bought, they sold, they planted, they builded; but the same day that Lot went out of Sodom it rained fire and brimstone from heaven, and destroyed them all. Even thus shall it be in the day when the Son of man is revealed. In that day, he which shall be upon the housetop, and his stuff in the house, let him not come down to take it away; and he that is in the field, let him likewise not return back. Remember Lot's wife" (Luke 17:28-32).

In this passage, the Lord Jesus was explaining that the days directly before His glorious and visible return would be like the days of Noah and of Lot. In the preceding chapter we considered the days of Noah, and here we will focus upon the days of Lot.

Doubtless there's no better comparison to Sodom and Gomorrah than our own day. But this fact is very serious, as the Apostle Peter wrote in 2 Peter 2:6, "And turning the cities of Sodom and Gomorrah into ashes condemned them with an overthrow, making them an ensample unto those that after should live ungodly." God pronounced His judgment upon Sodom and Gomorrah as a warning for the people who would live ungodly lives in the future. No matter how much they mock and think they can get away with sin, God's judgment will come upon them just as it did upon the people of Sodom and Gomorrah.

The Righteousness of Lot

I believe the Lord Jesus used Noah and Lot as an

example of the believing remnant of Jews who will live during the Great Tribulation. As it was for Noah and Lot in their time, so too will it be for the Jewish believers before Jesus returns. Both were an offense to their fellow man because they kept faith in God in the midst of apostasy.

In contrast to Noah, Lot is often regarded as a negative example. He is often portrayed as a child of God who compromised with the world, and lived, to a certain extent, in apostasy from God. For instance, the events in Genesis 13–19 have such headings in the Scofield Bible as, "Lot's first step in backsliding," "Lot's second step in backsliding," "The third step in Lot's backsliding," and "The last step in Lot's backsliding." Countless sermons have cast Lot in this negative light; in fact, I have even preached about him in this way. But is that really what the Bible says about Lot? In seeking to answer this question, I once again realized that as children of God we are often bound to believe what tradition tells us more often than we are committed to believe the truth in the Bible.

What Does the Bible Say About Lot?
• **Lot was spiritually comparable to Noah.** When the Lord Jesus spoke prophetically about the condition of mankind shortly before His return, He referred to Lot as being on the same level as Noah. He did not say anything negative about either of the men (Luke 17:26ff).

• **Lot was a godly man.** The Apostle Peter also

mentioned Noah and Lot in one breath: "For if God...spared not the old world, but saved Noah the eighth person, a preacher of righteousness, bringing in the flood upon the world of the ungodly; and turning the cities of Sodom and Gomorrah into ashes condemned them with an overthrow, making them an ensample unto those that after should live ungodly; and delivered just Lot, vexed with the filthy conversation of the wicked. (For that righteous man dwelling among them, in seeing and hearing, vexed his righteous soul from day to day with their unlawful deeds;) The Lord knoweth how to deliver the godly out of temptations, and to reserve the unjust unto the day of judgment to be punished" (2 Peter 2:4-9). Here Peter called Lot "just," "righteous," and "godly" without even mentioning that Lot had fallen into sin. In fact, Peter praised Lot as one who was saved from temptation because he had remained just and righteous. The word "godly" describes a person who follows the Lord wholeheartedly. In the Apostle Peter's second letter, we read: "Seeing then that all these things shall be dissolved, what manner of persons ought ye to be in all holy conversation and godliness" (2 Peter 3:11). The "holy conversation" and "godliness" are put on one and the same level here. Even Timothy was told, "Exercise thyself rather unto godliness" (1 Timothy 4:7).

• **Lot derived no pleasure in the sins of Sodom.** He did not tolerate them, nor did he partake of them. He suffered under the sinful behavior of the Sodomites.

The fact that Lot lived in Sodom was not a sin. Many Christians live in comparable cities around the world, where they work with unbelievers, travel with colleagues of other faiths, and go to the same vacation spots as people who do not follow God. Furthermore, most Christians have televisions in their homes, where they can watch graphic depictions of "Sodom and Gomorrah"–style living on any number of programs. Of course, having the television is not a sin; rather, what we choose to watch on TV determines whether we take part in sinful activity. It is not a sin to live in cities where various sins are blatantly practiced, but it can be extremely difficult to live in these cities and not partake in such sins. The scriptural text seems to assert that Lot was able to do this. Lot lived in the world, but he lived consciously with God. Also, the fact that Lot was referred to as a "sojourner" by the men of Sodom (Genesis 19:9) shows that he was not accepted because he did not live as they did.

• **Lot had a close relationship with his godly uncle, Abraham.** Up to the point of their separation, Lot had enjoyed a deep fellowship with Abraham. He stayed close to him and certainly had learned many valuable lessons from him. If Lot had possessed a sinful attitude, he most likely would not have sought close contact with his uncle; he would have tried to avoid him.

• **Lot didn't come up with the idea of going his own way into Sodom.** The suggestion to separate came from Abraham because their herds had become too large, "Is not the whole land before thee? Separate thyself, I pray thee, from me: if thou wilt take the left hand, then I will go to the right; or if thou depart to the right hand, then I will go to the left" (Genesis 13:9). Apparently Abraham was quite prepared to go to Sodom himself. Abraham gave Lot the choice. If Abraham had seen this as a sin, he would certainly have expressed himself differently.

• **Lot was spiritually discerning.** We find one clue of this in that he immediately recognized the angels when they came to visit him. Those who live with the Lord are able to recognize Him. Once he invited the angels into his home, the first thing Lot did was to bake unleavened bread and set it before them (Genesis 19:1-3). Did he do that as a man who had been living in sin? Certainly not. As a "righteous," "just," "godly" man, Lot sought fellowship with the Lord. This unleavened bread offers a picture of his inner attitude: Lot did not want to tolerate any sin.

• **Lot stood against evil.** When the sinners surrounded Lot's house, he immediately took his stand against the evil that they wanted to do to his guests (Genesis 19:4-7).

• **Lot was a sinner like the rest of us.** While the previous statements describe a man of faith and godliness, we cannot assume that Lot was without his own faults and sins. Remember how his daughters had seduced him when he was drunk, from which the sin of the Moabites and the Ammonites originated (Genesis 19:37-38)? However, Abraham did not make a better impression when he lied that his wife was his sister (Genesis 12:13; 20:2). Abraham's relationship with Hagar, his wife's handmaid, launched the Arabs, the descendants of Ishmael.

We should not embellish anything, nor should we read anything into the life of Lot that is not in the Bible. Instead, we should take the statements of Jesus and Peter seriously. They did not portray Lot as a half-hearted man who sat on the fence, but as a believer who was "righteous" and "godly" in the midst of an ungodly world.

Who among us can maintain that we live in this world as Lot lived in Sodom? Who among us is as vexed by the sin and unrighteousness of unbelievers as Lot had been? Who among us lives "without leaven" and resists evil like this man had? There will be people in Israel who will follow this example of Noah and Lot during the Great Tribulation (Revelation 7:14; 12:11; 14:4).

The Sins of Sodom

We do not need to list all the sins of our time. Every Christian should know we are living in a generation that has far exceeded the time of Sodom and Gomorrah in this respect.

I would however, like to mention just a few examples:

> • **Cloning.** On a German talk show American professor Panos Zavos presented the technology of cloning in a way that astounded the other par-

ticipants in the discussion. "We will create new people – no problem," he said. For him there can be no turning back. "The genie is out of the bottle. We can clone and we will clone."[1] A detailed report on cloning was featured in the German news magazine, *Focus*, entitled "Sin or goal of research?" That article described cloning as the greatest scientific sensation since the landing on the moon.[2] This technology is being made socially acceptable by films such as the one starring Arnold Schwarzenegger, appropriately entitled "The Sixth Day."

• **Entertainment.** "The standard of German television entertainment has sunk to unimaginable depths," reports an article. "On American television, scenes including violence have not decreased but there is three times the number of sex scenes. The barrier of disgust has never been as low."[3]

Here are some further examples:

• Faith in the Bible is publicly ridiculed.

• Christianity is decreasing to such an extent that in Germany, for instance, every third church is threatened with closure.

• Crosses have been banned from school classrooms in France and in parts of Germany, while religious symbols of other faiths are accepted.

• Homosexual "marriages" are permitted in Holland, and in some Scandinavian countries. In Switzerland, such "partnerships" are now able to be registered.

• The highest court in Israel has voted in favor of tax benefits for homosexual couples.

• In many cities of the world, large, well-organized parades of gays and lesbians have become common sights.

• Annually, about 50 million children are killed in their mother's wombs and their bodies are partially misused for scientific purposes.

• The number of crimes of violence has reached disturbing levels.

We are living in a time of total tolerance. Everything is tolerated; only Christians are not allowed to say that forgiveness of sin and salvation can only be found in Jesus Christ (John 14:6). The claim to absolutism is not tolerated.

The Sins of Sodom were Grievous

"And the LORD said, Because the cry of Sodom and Gomorrah is great, and because their sin is very grievous" (Genesis 18:20).

What did the people of Sodom and Gomorrah say about their way of life? They were "enlightened" people. A tolerant attitude was very important to them. Intolerance was sin. It is not important, however, what we call sin. It is not important whether we call certain activities "harmless" or "socially acceptable." The only thing that counts is how God views sin. His Word is very clear: "Whoremongers and adulterers God will judge" (Hebrews 13:4). No liar will enter the new Jerusalem: "And there shall in no wise enter into it any thing that defileth, neither whatsoever worketh abomination, or maketh a lie" (Revelation 21:27).

We can see how God views sin when we visit the Dead Sea, where the flourishing cities of Sodom and Gomorrah—which God turned into ashes and destroyed—once stood. Sin is always a serious subject to the Lord. This should make us fearful, for one day we will have to give an account of our lives to Him. Sin is so grave that God had no alternative but to lay it upon the back of His Son and let Him suffer its consequences for us.

God Does Not Tolerate Any Sin

We read about the people in Sodom: "But the men of Sodom were wicked and sinners before the LORD exceedingly" (Genesis 13:13).

As children many of us learned that the Bible is the subject and we are the objects. In other words, we were taught that the Bible is about us, rather than we being about the Bible. We cannot press God into our mold, however modern the world has become.

We have a thousand excuses and justifications for doing wrong. We justify sin by saying things like "Everyone does it," "It's not really that bad,". "We are living in different times now." But God has not changed, nor has the way that He sees sin. Joseph saw this and got his priorities right. When Potiphar's wife tried to seduce him, he reverently said, "How then can I do this great wickedness, and sin against God?" (Genesis 39:9).

Try telling someone that adultery or extra-marital relationships are wrong and that they are sins against God. They are likely to look at you in amazement or laugh at you.

The thief on the cross recognized and confessed at the end of his life, "we indeed justly; for we receive the due reward of our deeds: but this man [Jesus] hath done nothing amiss" (Luke 23:41).

No Sense of Right or Wrong

Abraham interceded for the sinful inhabitants of Sodom because he knew his nephew Lot lived there with his family. Abraham started to pray for 50 right-eous men (Genesis 18:24-25) and the Lord said to him, "If I find in Sodom fifty righteous within the city, then I will spare all the place for their sakes" (verse 26). Finally, Abraham pleaded, "Peradventure ten [righteous men] shall be found there," and his divine answer was, "I will not destroy it for ten's sake" (verse 32). On one hand, this sad fact reveals God's great mercy, but on the other hand, it reveals that the sinful Sodomites had no sense of right and wrong. They had defended their own righteousness, but there was no righteousness there in God's eyes.

Today there is a humanistic justice– and in some countries perhaps even a social justice. But biblical righteousness is nowhere to be found. That is why our world is growing spiritually darker. The following statement is true: "Humanity without divinity becomes bestiality." This leads directly to the coming anti-Christian kingdom.

Overturning All Values

When Lot and his two guests wanted to retire for the evening, we read: "But before they lay down, the men of the city, even the men of Sodom, compassed the house round, both old and young, all the people from every quarter: and they called unto Lot, and said unto him, Where are the men which came in to thee this night? Bring them out unto us, that we may know them" (Genesis 19:4-5). The meaning of these two verses is clear. It is the rejection of all the natural values that God has put in us. Today the opposite of normal is regarded as normal, and woe to anyone who speaks up against it!

Self-Justification

When Lot tried to protect his two guests from the immoral men of Sodom, they said, "Stand back. And they said again, This one fellow came in to sojourn, and he will needs be a judge: now will we deal worse with thee, than with them. And they pressed sore upon the man, even Lot, and came near to break the door" (Genesis 19:9).

Isn't this the way the present-day world speaks? It is not only about the renewal of right-wing radicalism and hostility towards foreigners. Above all, people seem to be accusing others in order to justify their own guilt. In the eyes of unbelievers, sin is not wrong-doing; sin is refusing to tolerate the beliefs and practices of others.

The Gravity of the Word of God

When Lot described the gravity of the situation to his sons-in-law, and tried to save them from the impending disaster, he said to them, "Up, get you out of this place: for the Lord will destroy this city." Then we read, "But he seemed as one that mocked unto his sons-in-law" (Genesis 19:14).

Worldly people often find it ridiculous—even a joke—to hear Christians talk about God's coming judgment, hell and the Rapture. But the worst thing is when a Christian no longer takes the Word of God seriously himself and keeps such truths to himself because he fears man.

Just as it once was in Noah's time, so it was also with Sodom. Once again it was not the masses that were right, but one man who believed the Word of God. It is tragic that Lot's sons-in-law did not accept the salvation offered them because they loved the darkness more than they loved the light. Yet God wanted to save them (compare Genesis 19:12-13).

Two Sides to the Near Future

Lot was saved. Sodom perished. The Apostle Peter wrote this about Lot: "The Lord knoweth how to deliver the godly out of temptations, and to reserve the unjust unto the day of judgment to be perished"

(2 Peter 2:9; compare Revelation 3:10). We also see this division in the book of Revelation: "He that is unjust, let him be unjust still: and he which is filthy, let him be filthy still: and he that is righteous, let him be righteous still" (Revelation 22:11).

Lot was "raptured" before God pronounced judgment upon Sodom and Gomorrah because he was godly. In other words, he had accepted salvation in faith and trusted the Word of God. We are made godly and kept from the coming judgment by faith in the Lord Jesus.

What about the others? In Luke 17:29, Jesus said, "But the same day that Lot went out of Sodom it rained fire and brimstone from heaven, and destroyed them all." The Church of Jesus Christ will be gone suddenly, and then unprecedented judgments will come upon this earth.

These two alternatives were clearly referred to by the Apostle Paul, when he wrote, "And to you who are troubled rest with us, when the Lord Jesus shall be revealed from heaven with his mighty angels, in flaming fire taking vengeance on them that know not God, and that obey not the gospel of our Lord Jesus Christ: who shall be punished with everlasting destruction from the presence of the Lord, and from the glory of his power; when he shall come to be glorified in his saints, and to be admired in all them that believe (because our testimony among you was believed) in that day" (2 Thessalonians 1:7-10).

The following quote appeared in a Christian magazine: "Christians as Jews believe in the grace of God. But they do not believe that there is no such thing as the wrath of God, because otherwise murderers would triumph over their victims. The grace and love of God do not make God a 'good Lord, who can do no harm,' but they show us the direction that God wants to take with man."[4]

My dear readers, you need to know one thing: God never intends to judge you. You are destined to be saved and forgiven. "For God hath not appointed us to wrath, but to obtain salvation by our Lord Jesus Christ" (1 Thessalonians 5:9).

The angels took Lot, his wife and his daughters by the hand: "And while he lingered, the men laid hold upon his hand, and upon the hand of his wife, and upon the hand of his two daughters; the LORD being merciful unto him: and they brought him forth, and set him without the city" (Genesis 19:16). God takes hold of our hands at Calvary. Everyone who grasps the hand of God in Jesus Christ will be saved. The Lord wants to spare you, and is extending His hand to you. Now it depends on whether you will take hold of His pierced hand and let Him save you. Take this step in unconditional faith in the atoning work of the Son of God on Calvary's cross!

To those of you who are born again, I want to say, "Of some have compassion, making a difference: and others save with fear, pulling them out of the fire; hating even the garment spotted by the flesh" (Jude 22-23). In other words, draw on all your natural and spiritual gifts to try to lead others to salvation, but do not allow yourselves to be contaminated by their sins.

1. *Privat Depesche* no.8/2001
2. *Focus* (German news magazine) 8/2001
3. *Idea Spektrum* (German Christian magazine) 6/2001
4. Walter Herrenbruck in *Idea Spektrum* 2/2001

Chapter 6

WATCH THEREFORE!

The Church of Jesus Christ is preparing for the return of the Lord. The danger of the endtimes is that the Church will be broken into.

" Watch therefore: for ye know not what hour your Lord doth come. But know this, that if the goodman [owner] of the house had known in what watch the thief would come, he would have watched, and would not have suffered his house to be broken up [into]. Therefore be ye also ready: for in such an hour as ye think not the Son of man cometh" (Matthew 24:42-44).

The word "watch" is mentioned a number of times in the Olivet Discourse, which makes it significant in view of endtime events. As the Church of Jesus Christ, we should find ourselves today, more than ever, in a state of continued preparation for the Lord's return, and be watchful in every respect, just as Jesus commanded: "Let your loins be girded about, and your lights burning; and ye yourselves like unto men that wait for their lord, when he will return from the wedding; that when he cometh and knocketh, they may open unto him immediately" (Luke 12:35-36). The people who lived during Jesus' time knew exactly what He meant when He said to "Let your loins be girded about." Oriental men wore long robes, which interfered with their movement. When they traveled or expected to be called to action at any moment, they bound up their robes so they would be ready.

In the same way, we should be preparing for the return of Jesus Christ. Those around us should be able to see that we are waiting for Jesus to return. We should never stop telling people about the sudden return of Jesus, even if some may laugh. We cannot make it clear enough that we are waiting for Jesus!

Grant Jeffrey wrote, "A prominent feature of a true disciple of Jesus is in the attitude he has of a faithful, waiting and watchful servant."[1] Dr. Klink expressed this as follows, "The continual expectation of the return of our Lord is a significant characteristic of early Christianity."[2]

The Past: A Warning for the Future

"Watch therefore: for ye know not what hour your Lord doth come. But know this, that if the goodman [owner] of the house had known in what watch the thief would come, he would have watched, and would not have suffered his house to be broken up" [into] (Matthew 24:42-43).

In the Olivet Discourse, Jesus was speaking on one hand about Jerusalem's imminent destruction, and on the other hand, about His return. This seems to also be the case here. Let's consider it more closely.

The Picture of the Past

It is striking that the Lord Jesus spoke in the past tense when He said, "If the goodman [owner] of the house had known." Why is this? Because He was referring to the predicted destruction of Jerusalem in 70 A.D. I believe the owner is a picture of the Jewish authorities in Jerusalem; the high priests, the Pharisees and the scribes. They had not watched nor did they recognize the signs of the times. The office of a watchman is described in Ezekiel 33:1ff. In the next chapter, the Lord spoke about the shepherds of Israel who did not watch over their flocks (chapter 34:1ff).

The spiritual authorities had already missed their cue when the Savior was born (Malachi 5:1). Although they could accurately identify where the Messiah would be born, they did not go there themselves. Later, the Lord rebuked them, saying, "When it is evening, ye say, It will be fair weather: for the sky is red. And in the morning, It will be foul weather today: for the sky is red and lowring. O ye hypocrites, ye can discern the face of the sky; but can ye not discern the signs of the times?" (Matthew 16:2-3). Yet there was no change for the better in them: "Though he had done so many miracles before them, yet they believed not on him" (John 12:37).

The "goodman" (owners) of the Jewish temple in Jerusalem did not watch. They did not recognize Jesus as the Messiah, and therefore they had to experience the worst. The "thief" came in 70 AD in the form of the Romans, and broke into the house so that not one stone remained upon the other. They took the treasures of the temple with them. Jesus' discourse on the Mount of Olives follows His words, "Behold, your house [the temple] is left unto you desolate" (Matthew 23:38). This describes an image much like the scenario after a thief breaks into a house and turns everything upside down.

Warning for the Future

The picture of the past becomes a warning for the

future. The hour of the Lord's return in power and great glory, together with His raptured and glorified Church, will be introduced by the Great Tribulation, which the Lord spoke about in great detail in Matthew 24.

At this time there will be many, mostly governing, people in Israel who are not watching and who do not have biblical faith. The result of this will be that the thief breaks in again.

The Lord will also come like a thief, suddenly, and without warning, "Behold, I come **as** a thief" (Revelation 16:15). But He is not the thief. The real thief is another, and he will appear on the scene **before** the Lord.

According to my understanding of Bible prophecy, the third temple will be built during the anti-Christian era, and the Antichrist will seat himself inside. He will "break into" it and establish the "abomination of desolation."

Prophetically speaking, the Antichrist is the thief of John 10, of whom the Lord Jesus said, "Verily, verily, I say unto you, He that entereth not by the door into the sheepfold, but climbeth up some other way, the same is a thief and a robber...The thief cometh not, but for to steal, and to kill, and to destroy: I am come that they might have life, and that they might have it more abundantly" (John 10:1, 10).

There is a "Savior of the world" and there will be a "murderer of the world." There is One who gave to the world, and there will be one who comes to steal from the world. Every person who is in Christ is one who has received; every person who is without Jesus is one who has been robbed of his life.

During an interview, a very wealthy man shared that he went to work each morning at 5 a.m. The first thing he did was read the obituaries in the newspaper. Then his secretary would bring him some tea or coffee, and he would work until 8 p.m. The reporter asked the wealthy man, "Why don't you fly to the Caribbean with your wife and take a three-month vacation?" He answered, "No, I can't do that anymore. I have to sit here and work." Although the man had everything as far as material wealth and possessions were concerned, he could not take a vacation and chose to work long hours each day. What a tragic and stolen life!

The meaning of life for a true Christian is to live with the Lord Jesus, of whom it is written, "This is the true God, and eternal life" (1 John 5:20). He said, "I am come that they might have life, and that they might have it more abundantly" (John 10:10). True life for a redeemed person takes place in the assurance that my sins have been forgiven. Jesus fully satisfied God's wrath against me. He is beside me in this life, and one day I will live with Him, the Son of God, in eternal glory! Let us receive from Jesus and not be robbed by God's opponent, living in continual fear of death.

When Will the Endtime Thief Come?

The Lord Jesus said, "But know this, that if the goodman [owner] had known in what watch the thief would come, he would have watched, and would not have suffered his house to be broken up" [into] (Matthew 24:43). The ticking of the clock is becoming louder. The hour of the "watch" is drawing near. The Apostle Paul wrote to the Christians in Thessalonica, "For yourselves know perfectly that the day of the Lord so cometh as a thief in the night" (1 Thessalonians 5:2). The Day of the Lord will begin with the Great Tribulation, which will bring in the Antichrist as a thief and a murderer.

Breaking into the Church

We do not find one sign in the Bible concerning the Rapture; that event will take place suddenly. The disciples did not know the exact time of Pentecost. The Lord Jesus simply said to them, "Ye shall be baptized with the Holy Ghost **not many days hence**" (Acts 1:5). Just as suddenly as the Holy Spirit came from heaven to the assembled disciples at Pentecost, He will also return to heaven with the Church of Jesus Christ at the Rapture. Then the entire earth will be covered in deep, spiritual darkness. The Antichrist, who will come on the scene at that time, will not make the world anti-Christian at his appearing, but will be crowned by a world that already is anti-Christian.

How is it today with the Church of Jesus Christ? Does the Church live in longing expectation for the return of Christ, or has it been broken into?

Breaking into the Household of the Church

"Know this, that if the goodman [owner] of the house had known in what watch the thief would come, he would have watched, and would not have suffered his house to be broken up" [into] (Matthew 24:43). This speaks of the owner of the house and the risk of failing to watch over the house. The Church is the "house," (i.e. the "temple" of the New Testament – 1 Peter 4:17, 1 Timothy 3:15). "Ye also, as lively stones, are built up a spiritual house," said Peter in 1 Peter 2:5. We run the risk of increased break-ins in the Church of Jesus Christ as we progress in endtime developments, because the owners of the house are not properly keeping watch.

Everything that contradicts the Bible belongs to the anti-Christian spirit, and this spirit is forcing its way into the Church like a thief in order to steal what is not being guarded. The owners of a church are the elders as leaders and shepherds. The Apostle Paul wrote, "For a bishop [overseer] must be blameless, as the steward of God" (Titus 1:7). The church leaders are stewards of God, stewards of spiritual matters and the gifts of a church. They watch over the rules the Holy Spirit has given the Church. For this reason elders were installed in the local churches (compare, for instance, Acts 20:28 and Titus 1:5).

I would like to follow that thought with an example. More and more churches are allowing women to administer the Lord's Supper. This is not consistent with biblical guidelines. We are not concerned with discrimination here, but with the keeping of the spiritual, God-given rules. Every person is considered equal before God. There is no difference where salvation is concerned, but there are where rules come into play. We must abide by rules in our everyday lives. Every citizen is equal where the state is concerned yet not everyone is a policeman. A policeman wearing an official uniform is authorized to direct the traffic. Under normal circumstances, an ordinary citizen in not permitted to take such matters upon himself. I only want to show here a tendency in endtime developments that has already reached the Church of Jesus Christ. The Church is being broken into according to the measure in which there is no watching for the Lord.

The Lord's Supper was instituted by the Lord Jesus, and was a modification of the Passover. At the Passover the father of the family, acting as the priest, had to slaughter the sacrificial lamb: "Speak ye unto all the congregation of Israel, saying, In the tenth day of this month they shall take to them every man a lamb, according to the house of their fathers, a lamb for an house" (Exodus 12:3). Here the father clearly presided over the family. Doesn't the celebration of the Lord's Supper belong to the household or stewardship of a church? It certainly does! That which Jesus told us to do through the apostles is carried out through the Lord's Supper: "this do in remembrance of me" (compare 2 Corinthians 11:23-25). This stewardship belongs exclusively to the offices of elders and deacons.

Breaking into Our Personal Sanctification

Sanctification is a part of our personal watchfulness, so that the thief cannot break in and steal things that have been sanctified to the Lord. Nothing serves our personal sanctification more than the living expectation of the return of Jesus Christ (Romans 13:11-12). This is why the Apostle Paul wrote to Timothy: "These things write I unto thee, hoping to come unto thee shortly: but if I tarry long, that thou mayest know how thou oughtest to behave thyself in the house of God, which is the church of the living God, the pillar and ground of the truth" (1 Timothy 3:14-15).

The following anecdote is reported of Martin Luther: One night the reformer was visited by the devil, who woke him and asked, "Does Luther live here?" Martin Luther is said to have said to him, "No, Christ lives here!" whereupon the devil fled. This is an example of spiritual warfare. Now let us ask ourselves how should we behave in the house of God, the Church of Jesus Christ? The Lord Jesus said, "**Watch** therefore: for ye know not what hour your Lord doth come" (Matthew 24:42). What does He mean by "watching"?

"To Watch" Means to Purge the Leaven

Leaven (yeast) is a picture of sin and its devastating ability to spread. Before every Passover feast, all leaven had to be removed from the houses of the Israelites (Exodus 12:15). The women were very careful to do this; they searched the entire house with candles into the farthest corners to find the tiniest bit of leaven and to remove it.

First Corinthians 5:6-8 explains, "Know ye not that a little leaven leaveneth the whole lump? Purge out therefore the old leaven, that ye may be a new lump, as ye are unleavened. For even Christ our Passover is sacrificed for us: therefore let us keep the feast, not with old leaven, neither with the leaven of malice and wickedness; but with the unleavened bread of sincerity and truth." A little leaven, tolerating just a little sin (be it envy, malice, lying, etc.), can infect a person, even an entire church.

The blood of Jesus Christ cleansed every born-again person at his or her conversion, but we must be careful to not become recontaminated with "leaven." Sin will break into our homes and rob us of the Holy Spirit's peace, joy and power if we are not careful. The Bible says that everyone who has the hope of Jesus' return purifies himself, just as He is pure (1 John 3:3).

Removing the leaven also means that we must watch over the unity within the Church: "I therefore, the prisoner of the Lord, beseech you that ye walk worthy of the vocation wherewith ye are called, with all lowliness and meekness, with longsuffering, forbearing one another in love; endeavouring to keep the unity of the Spirit in the bond of peace" (Ephesians 4:1-3).

"To Watch" Means To Walk in the Light

What night-watchman would go on duty without the help of a good torch? What miner would go down into a mine without a lamp? Fewer break-ins occur in houses that are brightly lit

How often does the Bible instruct us to be watchful and to walk in the light? "Walk while ye have the light, lest darkness come upon you" (John 12:35). Thieves usually break in when it is dark. If it is dark in our hearts, then it will be easier for the thief to steal from us. But the thief will not dare to break in if our hearts are full of the light of Jesus, and if we are full of the Holy Spirit, because he would be discovered immediately and would be cast out. Romans 13:11-14 explains what it means to walk in the light: "And that, knowing the time, that now it is high time to awake out of sleep: for now is our salvation nearer than when we believed. The night is far spent, the day is at hand: let us therefore cast off the works of darkness, and let us put on the armour of light. Let us walk honestly, as in the day; not in rioting and drunkenness, not in chambering and wantonness, not in strife and envying. But put ye on the Lord Jesus Christ, and make not provision for the flesh, to fulfil the lusts thereof."

"To Watch" Means To Abide in Jesus

The Son of God is the protector of our lives. That is why we should put Him on like clothing, "put ye on the Lord Jesus Christ" (Romans 13:14). In Him, we are completely protected from every sin. In and through Jesus we have and continue to have victory. Not to watch means not to be in Jesus.

We will be victorious when the Lord controls our lives through His Spirit. Then we can resist the devil and reject sin, and we will wait longingly for the appearance of the Lord. What does it mean to abide in Jesus (John 15:4)? It means that by faith I accept what I have in Him. In practical terms, this can be that I often say to the Lord Jesus, "I thank You that in accordance with Your Word I am already crucified, dead, buried and risen again to new life with You. I believe, according to Romans 6, that I have died to sin." In this way, we are abiding in Christ. The Apostle Paul testified, "I am crucified with Christ: nevertheless I live; yet not I, but Christ liveth in me: and the life which I now live in the flesh I live by the faith of the Son of God, who loved me, and gave himself for me" (Galatians 2:20). Jesus is Savior and Lord of His own. If we fall and confess to Him our failure, He will not leave us lying there, but will help us up again.

If we do not abide in Jesus, the thief will rob us of our assurance of salvation and victory. This is why we are told in 1 John 2:28, "And now, little children, abide in him; that, when he shall appear, we may have confidence, and not be ashamed before him at his coming."

The Church of Jesus Christ is preparing for His return. But for this very reason there is great danger

91

that it will be broken into. Therefore, let us be watchful in our personal wait for the return of Jesus, and live our lives accordingly!

1. *When the Trumpet Sounds* by Thomas Ice and Timothy Demy, Copyright 1995, Harvest House Publishers.
2. Ibid

Chapter 7

THE CASE FOR BIBLICAL PROPHECY

Matthew 24:44-51 can be interpreted as Jesus' summation of the preceding statements in the same chapter. In His speech, the Lord brings His statements concerning the end-times to a head, and calls upon us to be watchful. Part of this is that we concern ourselves intensively with His prophetic Word, and see that others also hear it.

" Therefore be ye also ready; for in such an hour as ye think not the Son of man cometh. Who then is a faithful and wise servant, whom his lord hath made ruler over his household, to give them meat in due season? Blessed is that servant, whom his lord when he cometh shall find so doing. Verily I say unto you, That he shall make him ruler over all his goods. But and if that evil servant shall say in his heart, My lord delayeth his coming; And shall begin to smite his fellow servants, and to eat and drink with the drunken; the lord of that servant shall come in a day when he looketh not for him, and in an hour that he is not aware of, and shall cut him asunder, and appoint him his portion with the hypocrites; there shall be weeping and gnashing of teeth" (Matthew 24:44-51).

This passage speaks about a servant with the specific task of providing food for the members of his master's household. Faithfully fulfilling this task to his master's satisfaction would earn the servant a reward.

What does the phrase "meat in due season" mean? It is the proclamation of the prophetic Word of God, the tireless pointing to the return of Jesus. The parallel text of Luke 12:42 uses the phrase, "to give them their portion of meat in due season."

We must consider these verses in connection with Jesus' statements recorded in Matthew 24, where the Lord spoke exclusively about His return and gave us a prophetic view of the last days. In this context He spoke of the necessity of spreading the prophetic

Word as "meat in due season." The clearer the signs become, the more important it is to do the right thing. The Lord emphasized that He was speaking about our inner preparation for His return with His words about the evil servant, who said, "in his heart, My lord delayeth his coming" (verse 48). We are concerned here with the expectation of His soon return.

Proclaiming the prophetic Word of God is not the hobby of certain preachers; it is an urgent responsibility assigned by the Lord Himself, "We have also a more sure word of prophecy; whereunto ye do well that ye take heed" (2 Peter 1:19).

The Literal Meaning

According to my understanding of Scripture, the "faithful servant" refers to the faithful remnant of Jews who will come to believe in the Messiah, Jesus Christ, during the 70th week of years. When the Church of Jesus Christ has been raptured, the seed that has been sown by the Messianic Jews in Israel today will spring up. The 144,000 sealed Jews of Revelation 7:4ff and the two witnesses of Revelation 11:3ff will appear on the scene and proclaim the Old and the New Testament in Israel. Then a revival will take place. Many Jewish people will turn to Jesus Christ. These believers out of Israel will prove their faithfulness to the Lord during the hard times of the Great Tribulation and teach their Jewish people about the imminent return of Christ. They will give them the "meat" of the prophetic Word. When divine judgment comes upon the earth, they will bring the right "meat in due season" from the book of Revelation and say, "See, the prophecies are being fulfilled!"

When the Lord returns at the end of these seven years, He will reward the Jewish remnant by making it "ruler over all his goods" (Matthew 24:47). His "goods" will extend over the entire earth and the nations in the Millennium of Peace.

I believe the "evil servant" refers to the apostate Jews of the last seven years. A great division will take place within the Jewish people. Many people will radically turn away from the faith of the fathers (2 Peter 3:4) and enter a covenant with the Antichrist (Daniel 9:27). They will betray their own brothers by not believing in the return of the Messiah, and will "smite" their fellow countrymen (Matthew 24:49). The love they have in their hearts will grow cold because lawlessness through the "lawless one" will reach its full effect (2 Thessalonians 2:7-8). Matthew 24:12 states, "Because iniquity shall abound, the love of many shall wax cold." Who are the "many" referred to here? Not the world, which has no divine love in any case. Nor is it the Church, which already will have been raptured before the Great Tribulation begins. No, the "many" refers to the masses of Jewish people, for Matthew 24 points to the situation of the Jews directly preceding the visible return of Jesus Christ. Many will fall away from the faith of the fathers. Even today, the majority of Jews is not seeking God, but is treading upon a secular path, and is prepared to accept almost any kind of peace.

The term "many" is derived from Daniel 9:27, where it is written, "And he shall confirm the covenant with many for one week [seven years]: and in the midst of the week he shall cause the sacrifice and the oblation to cease, and for the overspreading of abominations he shall make it desolate, even until the consummation, and that determined shall be poured upon the desolate." On the other hand, Daniel 12:3 states this about the "faithful servant": "And they that be wise shall shine as the brightness of the firmament; and they that turn many to righteousness as the stars for ever and ever." The "faithful servants" will proclaim the Gospel, the righteousness of Jesus and His imminent return, to the "many" (the Jewish people). But many of these people will not believe, and will turn to the false Messiah.

Those among the Jews who behave like "evil servants" during the Great Tribulation up until the return of Jesus, and will not be convicted of their evil deeds, will not partake in the Millennium of Peace. The Lord Jesus expressed this sentiment with these serious words: "and shall cut him asunder, and appoint him his portion with the hypocrites: there shall be weeping and gnashing of teeth" (Matthew 24:51). Ezekiel already prophesied in this connection, "they shall not enter into the land of Israel" (compare Ezekiel 20:37-38). That which Peter prophesied also applies to apostate Jews, "that there shall come in the last days scoffers, walking after their own lusts, and saying, Where is the promise of his coming? For since the fathers fell asleep, all things continue as they were from the beginning of creation" (2 Peter 3:3-4, compare also Ezekiel 12:21ff). The Apostle Peter's two letters address Jews (1 Peter 1:1 and 2 Peter 3:1), and the word "fathers" refers to the patriarchs of Judaism.

Application to Our Time

"Who then is a faithful and wise servant, whom his lord hath made ruler over his household, to give them meat in due season? Blessed is that servant, whom his lord when he cometh shall find so doing" (Matthew 24:45-46).

What is "meat in due season"?

1. I consider the phrase "meat in due season" as a warning to the Church of Jesus Christ. In view of current events, we must take heed that we do not disregard what is relevant and proclaim what the Spirit wants to tell us. To this belongs the entire counsel of God, of course, particularly that of biblical prophecy.

The recent upheavals in Israel, the attack on America, the increase of terrorism, the threats of war and the reports about war, the global economic crisis, increasing lawlessness, etc. are all preludes to the Great Tribulation, which will lead to the return of Jesus Christ.

It seems that we are standing at the threshold of the

birth pangs of judgment, which are becoming stronger and stronger and occurring at shorter intervals. The prophet Haggai summed it up as follows, "For thus saith the LORD of hosts; Yet once, it is a little while, and I will shake the heavens, and the earth, and the sea, and the dry land; and I will shake all nations, and the desire of all nations shall come" (Haggai 2:6-7).

Is there good news for our planet, which is being afflicted by upheavals of the most terrible kind? Is there a message for our world, which is suffering because of war and terror, and in which all peace efforts fail and the circumstances get worse? Yes. The message is that Jesus is coming! He is the only hope for our world, a hope that all creation longs for (Romans 8:22-23).

2. I also understand that in accordance with 2 Peter 1:19, we should look upon the prophetic Word as "meat" for our time, and concern ourselves with it.

At the beginning of the Revelation of Jesus Christ, we read: "Blessed is he that readeth, and they that hear the words of this prophecy, and keep those things which are written therein: for the time is at hand" (Revelation 1:3). At the end of that book we read, "Behold, I come quickly: blessed is he that keepeth the sayings of the prophecy of this book" (Revelation 22:7).

3. I believe the phrase "meat in due season" also

points to the signs of the times, and to the fact that we should correctly interpret them so we can tell people what they must do. The faithful servant knew what meat he had to provide at what time.

When it came time to make David king of Hebron, we read: "And of the half tribe of Manasseh eighteen thousand, which were expressed by name, to come and make David king [a picture of the return of Jesus]. And of the children of Issachar, which were men that had understanding of the times, to know what Israel ought to do" (1 Chronicles 12:31-32).

John Wesley wrote a letter to his brother Charles in 1755, in which he expressed the right attitude concerning the return of Christ:

> I know that many have been mistaken about the year of His return, but should we be unwise on account of the presumptuous claims of such people? Just because they say, 'today,' should we say, 'never,' and, 'peace, peace' when we should be full of expectation?[1]

Gerard Kramer wrote, "We should perhaps ask ourselves why we are not more excited about the return of Jesus Christ."[2] William McDonald said on this same subject, "It is not enough for us to cling to the truth of His return; this truth must grip us." Johannes Calvin said, "The most important thing for believers should be to concentrate their thoughts completely on His return."[3] And the Apostle Paul's spiritual testament was, "I have fought a good fight, I have finished my course, I have kept the faith:

Henceforth there is laid up for me a crown of right-eousness, which the Lord, the righteous judge, shall give me at that day: and not to me only, but unto all them also that love his appearing" (2 Timothy 4:7-8).

What Does "Meat in Due Season" Produce?

1. The phrase, "meat in due season" makes us aware of our living hope and keeps it alive in us. The Apostle Paul wrote this description of the Rapture: "that ye sorrow not, even as others which have no hope…Then we which are alive and remain shall be caught up together with them in the clouds, to meet the Lord in the air: and so shall we ever be with the Lord. Wherefore comfort one another with these words" (1 Thessalonians 4:13, 17-18). In other words, "You may be experiencing tribulation, fear and tears, but be of good cheer; it will not always be like this! Jesus is coming! He will wipe away the tears from the faces of His redeemed (Revelation 7:17; 21:4). Then you will rejoice with unspeakable and glorified joy over the One "whom having not seen, ye love; in whom, though now ye see him not, yet believ-ing, ye rejoice with joy unspeakable and full of glory" (1 Peter 1:8).

Gerard Kramer asked: "Is this hope really alive in us? We should actually wake up every morning with the thought, 'Maybe it will be today!' and before we go to sleep, 'Maybe this night!' Do we think during the day that the Lord could suddenly call us to meet Him in the air? …Or does this all sound a bit exaggerated, even a little strange? The daily expectation of the Lord Jesus should be the normal thing for every Christian."[4]

Many Christians do not even include the possibility of the Rapture in their faith lives! They toss the topic aside, saying, "My Lord delays His coming." They have forgotten, or maybe they do not know, that the Bible does not give us any signs that will precede the Rapture of the Church; all the signs given in Scripture point to the time before Christ's return in great power and glory. If we are recognizing some of the signs of the times today, then the Rapture must be very close, for this will take place before the Great Tribulation. What does the return of Jesus mean to our churches? Unfortunately, the topic is seldom even mentioned in the pulpit. It's a rare Sunday morning that finds a pastor asking his congregation: "Are you ready for Jesus' coming?"

In a sermon on comfort, Martin Luther said that the hope of the return of Christ is an absolute necessity for a Christian: "If you are not filled with a burning desire for this day, you can never pray the Lord's Prayer...If you believed it, you would of a necessity long for it with all your heart; if you do not have this longing, you are not a Christian, nor can you glory in your faith."[5]

These words of Luther are commented on as follows:

"In the whole of the New Testament we continually read admonitions to make the return of our Lord the central point of our spiritual lives. This blessed hope of the Rapture should by no means be an interesting secondary topic for the study of the prophetic Word, but a pillar of our spiritual lives."[6]

2. "Meat in due season" is the strongest motivation for sanctification. Why did Enoch live in such close contact with his God? We read of him, "And Enoch walked with God: and he was not, for God took him" (Genesis 5:24). We find the answer in Jude 14, "And Enoch also, the seventh from Adam, prophesied of these, saying, Behold, the Lord cometh with ten thousands of his saints." Enoch knew and proclaimed the Lord's return thousands of years ago. This knowledge made a different man of him.

One prominent sign of a true Christian is the attitude of a faithful, waiting and watchful servant. Floyd Elmore said, "The only possibility for the Church of Jesus Christ to avoid the world and to become truly one is in a working of the Spirit through the proclamation of the Word, and a life in expectation of the return of the Lord."[7]

Dr. Kling wrote: "True waiting for the coming of Christ does not make us lazy or unproductive, but fills us with great zeal to employ and to improve every spiritual gift continually in an appropriate way."[8]

To long for the return of Jesus inevitably has an effect on our daily lives: "Seeing then that all these things shall be dissolved, what manner of persons ought ye to be in all holy conversation and godliness, looking for and hasting unto the coming of the day of God...Wherefore, beloved, seeing that ye look for such things, be diligent that ye may be found of him in peace, without spot, and blameless" (2 Peter 3:11-12, 14).

"We shall see him as he is. And every man that hath this hope in him purifieth himself, even as he is pure" (1 John 3:2-3). Whoever thinks that he or she can be purified without the living expectation of Jesus' return is in grave error, for true purification or sanctification comes through the Spirit of God. John 16:13 tells us what He does: "When he, the Spirit of truth, is come, he will guide you into all truth: for he shall not speak of himself; but whatsoever he shall hear, that shall he speak: and he will shew you things to come."

Knowledge of biblical prophecy brings great blessing to believers:

• It brings joy in the midst of affliction (2 Corinthians 4:17).

• It demands purity and a holy life (1 John 3:3).

• It is, like all the rest of the Scripture, profitable for the Christian life (2 Timothy 3:16-17).

• It teaches us about life after death (2 Corinthians 5:8).

• It teaches us about the end of the world.

• It proves the reliability of the entire Bible, for the many exactly fulfilled promises are not a product of chance.

• It leads our hearts to worship God, who has history in His hand and will fulfill His will.

Ignoring the teachings of prophecy leads to the loss of these blessings.

The Faithful and Wise Servant

Matthew wrote about the faithful and wise servant: "Who then is a faithful and wise servant, whom his lord hath made ruler over his household, to give them meat in due season? Blessed is that servant, whom his lord when he cometh shall find so doing" (Matthew 24:45-46).

Faithfulness and wisdom are demonstrated in the expectation and proclamation of the return of Jesus. I have a practical question to interject here: When do we need to eat? Daily. Don't we prepare for meals every day by purchasing the food, setting the table, cooking the meals, calling our family and friends to the table, and serving the meals? It is just as important for us to be busy and active in preparing for Jesus' return on a daily basis.

The Lord hinted that He wants to find His servants doing such things (verse 46). We cannot serve the "meat in due season" at some times and not at other times. We need to do it every day!

The Evil Servant

The evil servant is described in Matthew 24:48-49: "But and if that evil servant shall say in his heart, My lord delayeth his coming; and shall begin to smite his fellow servants, and to eat and drink with the drunken." Unfaithfulness and evil are demonstrated by those who do not expect the return of Jesus daily.

The evil servant also thinks of eating, but from a different aspect. While the wise servant has food for the future in mind, the evil servant concentrates on the present, like the people in the days before the Flood: "They were eating and drinking, marrying and giving in marriage, until the day that Noe entered into the ark" (Matthew 24:38).

What are you concentrating on other than your everyday responsibilities? Are you anticipating the future? Are you looking forward to the kingdom of God? Are you preparing for the Rapture? Are you putting all your energy into loving the appearing of Jesus? Is this something that you pray to the Lord about? Do you have a burden in your heart for those around you? Do you tell them and show them that the Lord Jesus is coming, and that His prophetic Word is being fulfilled?

Or are you more concerned about yourself? Do all your thoughts and actions revolve around you, the present, your career, and your children? Are you always trying to find fault with those around you? Do you try to make yourself look good and put others down? Do you slander your neighbor with evil words, or talk about them behind their backs?

Many people say nobody can know the day or the hour of Jesus' return (Matthew 24:36) and leave it at that. This is true, but the Lord does not want us to use those words as a comfortable cushion of complacency. We can know a lot about the return of Jesus in theory without expecting it.

Evil servants do not think that the Lord will not return. They, too, reckon with His return. But they think that it won't happen for a long time. They may not say it publicly, but perhaps only mention it in the company of his family or friends. They believe that many other things have to take place before the Lord can return. Perhaps they even refer to certain Bible texts to "prove" that the Lord cannot come yet.

Such people have been deceived by the enemy because the Lord's return will be a surprise: "The lord of that servant shall come in a day when he looketh not for him, and in an hour that he is not aware of" (Matthew 24:50).

How far you have progressed in your sanctification is revealed by your inner expectation. Are you waiting for Jesus with a burning heart, or are you indifferent? Do not speak about sanctification if you are not longingly waiting for Him. Dr. Wim Malgo once wrote, "If you have really turned from idols to serve the living God, then it cannot be otherwise than that you are waiting for Him." The Lord Jesus rejoices over His servants who wait for Him longingly and who give their fellow Christians "meat in due season": "Blessed is that servant, whom his lord when he cometh shall find so doing"

(Matthew 24:46). It is high time for us to arise and to do that!

1 *When the Trumpet Sounds* by Thomas Ice and Timothy Demy, Copyright 1995, Harvest House Publishers
2 *Fest und Treu*
3 *When the Trumpet Sounds*
4 Ibid
5 Ibid
6 Ibid
7 Ibid
8 Ibid

Chapter 8

THE CRY AT MIDNIGHT

The goal of this chapter is to portray Jesus' parable
concerning the 10 virgins from a different aspect than usual.
Certainly these words from our Lord can be applied in an
evangelistic sense, and to the Rapture. But I believe a deeper
meaning can be applied.

" Then shall the kingdom of heaven be likened unto ten virgins, which took their lamps, and went forth to meet the bridegroom. And five of them were wise, and five were foolish. They that were foolish took their lamps, and took no oil with them: but the wise took oil in their vessels with their lamps. While the bridegroom tarried, they all slumbered and slept. And at midnight there was a cry made, Behold, the bridegroom cometh; go ye out to meet him. Then all those virgins arose, and trimmed their lamps. And the foolish said unto the wise, Give us of your oil; for our lamps are gone out. But the wise answered, saying, Not so; lest there be not enough for us and you: but go ye rather to them that sell, and buy for yourselves. And while they went to buy, the bridegroom came; and they that were ready went in with him to the marriage: and the door was shut. Afterward came also the other virgins, saying, Lord, Lord, open to us. But he answered and said, Verily I say unto you, I know you not. Watch therefore, for ye know neither the day nor the hour wherein the Son of man cometh" (Matthew 25:1-13).

What Is a Parable?

Parables were stories the Lord used from daily life to make spiritual application and to make important truths understandable. Parables must not be taken out of context. Therefore, the parable of the 10 virgins belongs within the framework of Jesus' endtime speech, which concerns the Jewish people. It is about events that take place before and during the revelation of the Lord in Israel — at midnight.

In the parable of the 10 virgins, the Lord Jesus used the customs practiced at a Jewish or Oriental wedding and applied them spiritually to the endtimes.

To What Does the Parable of the 10 Virgins Refer?

Matthew 25:1 reads: "Then shall the kingdom of heaven be likened unto ten virgins, which took their lamps, and went forth to meet the bridegroom." This introduction reveals that the parable of the 10 virgins refers to the preceding events in Matthew 24, and draws our attention to a new event during this time: the climax, the end of the Great Tribulation, at midnight.

The word "then" points to the last events of the Great Tribulation on earth, when the Son of Man returns to establish a new era at the beginning of His reign: "Then shall the kingdom of heaven be likened unto ten virgins."

The people of Israel were at the center of prophecy in the Olivet Discourse, and that remains the case in Matthew 25. We are still concerned with the disciples' question about the sign of His coming and the completion of the age, when the Messianic rule over Israel begins (Matthew 24:3). Jesus did not refer here to the Rapture, but to His return in great power and glory for the completion of this age and the beginning of His reign (Matthew 24:27, 30). The Lord described the conditions concerning the land and the people, which precede this new era—namely, the Great Tribulation.

The Lord Jesus spoke vaguely about the Rapture on the evening before He was crucified (John 14:1-3), but not in the Olivet Discourse, which had taken place a few days earlier.

I believe Matthew 24 refers to the Jewish people. For instance:

• "Ye shall be hated of all nations" (verse 9) – The Jewish people, not the Church, will be hated by all nations (compare Psalm 83:3-5; Daniel 3:8, 6:12,14 and Psalm 44:23).

• "The abomination of desolation...in the holy place" (verse 15) – This refers to the Jewish temple, which has not yet been built.

• "Spoken of by Daniel the prophet" – Daniel spoke about the Jewish people, not the Church.

• "Then let them which be in Judea flee into the mountains" (verse 16) –This clearly refers to the Jewish land.

• "Let him which is on the housetop not come down" – Houses in the Orient typically had flat roofs.

• "But pray ye that your flight be not...on the sabbath day" (verse 20) – The Church was not commanded to keep the Sabbath (Colossians 2:16-17).

• "This generation shall not pass" (verse 34) – This refers to the generation of the Jews. The Church is not a generation.

Where Is the Bride?

When we carefully read the parable of the 10 virgins, notice it mentions the arrival of the bridegroom, the virgins (wedding guests) who were expecting him, and a Marriage Supper (Matthew 25:10). However, there is no mention of a bride. Why not? I believe there are two reasons for this:

1. The fact that the Bride, who represents the Church of Jesus Christ, is not mentioned is one more proof that the "Body of Christ" (Ephesians 1:22-23) is not the object or content of the message of Matthew 24 and 25. It is the people of Israel (the virgins).

2. The Church of Jesus Christ is not mentioned because it will be taken to heaven as the Bride of the Lamb before the Great Tribulation, "from the hour of temptation, which shall come upon all the world" (Revelation 3:10). At the latest, this will happen before the events of Matthew 24:15 take place, and it will return with Jesus.

Why will the Church be raptured beforehand? Because the spiritual restoration of Israel will take place during that time (Ezekiel 36 and 37). This can only happen after the Church Age has come to an end and the Church has been raptured (Romans 11:25-26). According to Galatians 3:28, Israel will not be spiritually restored while the Church remains on earth because there is no difference between Jews who believe in Jesus and Gentiles. Every person who believes in Jesus belongs to the Church and will be raptured. After the Rapture, the people of Israel will become the focus of God's attention, and there will be a difference between believing Jews and believing Gentiles (Revelation 7:4-9ff).

113

The Bible gives us further explanation in other places:

• We read in Revelation 19:7-8 about the Bride, who is already in heaven at the marriage feast: "Let us be glad and rejoice, and give honour to him: for the marriage of the Lamb is come, and his wife hath made herself ready. And to her was granted that she should be arrayed in fine linen, clean and white: for the fine linen is the righteousness of saints."

• The following verse mentions the invitation to the Marriage Supper: "And he saith unto me, Write, Blessed are they which are called unto the marriage supper of the Lamb. And he saith unto me, These are the true sayings of God" (verse 9). Notice that the time for the marriage has come, but the Marriage Supper has not yet taken place; only the invitation to it is mentioned.

• The Marriage Supper will probably take place on this earth, because the Lord returns to the earth with His Bride after the mention of the Marriage Supper: "And I saw heaven opened, and behold a white horse; and he that sat upon him was called Faithful and True, and in righteousness he doth judge and make war...And the armies which were in heaven followed him upon white horses, clothed in fine linen, white and clean" (Revelation 19:11, 14). Then He enters the place where the Marriage Supper will be served, and the celebration will take place.

I imagine the sequence of events to be as follows:

1. The Church, as the Bride of the Lord Jesus, will

be raptured from the earth. It will then be united with the heavenly Bridegroom in the clouds of heaven. Then the Bride will be led into the Father's house (John 14:1-3). The wedding will take place there (Revelation 19:7-8).

2. During the Great Tribulation, a remnant of the Jewish people is being prepared for the Marriage Supper in the Millennium of Peace: "Blessed are they which are called unto the marriage supper of the Lamb" (Revelation 19:9).

3. Then the Lord Jesus will return in glory, accompanied by His Bride, to celebrate the Marriage Supper (Revelation 19:11-16, compare also 1 Thessalonians 3:13). I believe this Marriage Supper will mark the beginning of the Millennium of Peace and will express the joy and blessings of this millennium.

There were three stages of a marriage in biblical times: First, contact was made between the parents of the bride, the bride's parents, and the bridegroom. At this point, the bridegroom would pay the bride price. The Lord Jesus paid the bride price for His Church with His own blood. Second, the bridegroom needed time to prepare the place where the new couple would live. Normally he would return about a year later to take his bride home. This stage corresponds with the Rapture of the Church to the Father's house (John 14:1-3). Third, the marriage took place. This is when the bridegroom appeared with the bride and welcomed the guests. This stage points to the return of Jesus with the Church.

The Lord Jesus spoke in a parable about the invitation to the marriage and the Marriage Supper: "And when the king came in to see the guests, he saw there a man which had not on a wedding garment: and he saith unto him, Friend, how camest thou in hither not having a wedding garment? And he was speechless. Then said the king to the servants, Bind him hand and foot, and take him away, and cast him into outer darkness; there shall be weeping and gnashing of teeth" (Matthew 22:11-13). This cannot refer to heaven, because no one who does not belong to Jesus Christ will enter heaven. I believe the Lord was referring to His future kingdom on earth, from which many people will be excluded. There will be many in Israel who will not come to a living faith in the Messiah Jesus during the Great Tribulation.

As in the parable of the 10 virgins, we are obviously concerned with a Marriage Supper. The union of the Church with the Lord Jesus must already have taken place. It is not necessarily significant, but interesting, that the Syrian translation of the Bible and the Vulgate (the Latin translation of the Bible) says, "the bridegroom came with his bride." [1] It is certainly significant, however, that the Lord Jesus said to the Jews, "And ye yourselves like unto men that wait for their lord, when he will return from the wedding; that when he cometh and knocketh, they may open unto him immediately" (Luke 12:36). Christ spoke about a wedding that has already taken place, and of His return from it. The command to watch is given to the Jews on earth at that time and they should prepare for this event.

Let us summarize: The marriage will take place in heaven; the Marriage Supper will take place on the earth. The marriage concerns the Church; the Marriage Supper (invited guests) refers to Israel (Matthew 22:1-14; Luke 14:16-24).

What is the Warning for the Church?

If the Church already will be in heaven at the time—as mentioned in Matthew 25—to return with the Lord Jesus as His Bride, the cry at midnight—"Behold, the bridegroom cometh!" (verse 6)—is even more urgent. The signs of the times speak an unmistakable language. The clearer the events of Matthew 24 cast their shadows ahead of them, the closer we must be to the Rapture of the Bride.

For instance, Matthew 24:6-7 says, "And ye shall hear of wars and rumours of wars: see that ye be not troubled: for all these things must come to pass, but the end is not yet. For nation shall rise against nation, and kingdom against kingdom: and there shall be famines, and pestilences, and earthquakes, in divers places." We hear about wars and rumors of wars through various media today.

• The title of one press report: More wars, greater famines and mass flights out of many lands. [1]

• The "Coalition for the International World Court of Judgment" summarized in a statistic that the world has experienced more than 250 wars in the past 50 years [since the founding of the state of Israel]. More

117

than 86 million civilians have been killed; that is more than the casualties from World Wars I and II combined. More than 170 million people have been robbed of their rights, their possessions and their dignity. [2]

• Rumors of war are rampant. The media is filled with reports of war and terror. There is great fear of nuclear rearmament in Arab countries such as Syria, Libya, Iran, and North Korea. India and Pakistan are armed to the teeth and are continually at odds with one another despite efforts to achieve peace: "Nation shall rise against nation."

• In a daily newspaper: "The British Ministry of Defence has published secret documents over the past five years containing instructions for building atomic bombs...They contain a list of all the components required, up to the amount of plutonium necessary. The documents, previously kept secret, are now open to all in the British national archives. Terrorist organizations could use these to produce lesser arms — if they could obtain the plutonium."[3]

• Swiss general Hans Bachofner wrote this concerning rumors of war: "Now the drums of war are heard beyond our borders. The overwhelming peace rhetoric of the past ten years has turned into a no less overwhelming war rhetoric. The peace soldiers, who created and protected peace, the peace efforts and peace processes are being ousted by elite soldiers, Clausewitz quotations, war reports and reports of victories. Have they any idea where they are leading?" [4]

• Endless unrest in the Middle East simmers before

our eyes. The Israeli/Palestinian conflict, particularly the tirades of hatred coming from the Palestinians, continues. The situation in Afghanistan continues to smolder. Tension in Kosovo remains explosive. The USA is rearming at an alarming rate. Russia is looking to regain its status as a superpower. Terrorism has reached international proportions. Atomic weapons have become easier to obtain. The nations are already gathering in "Babylon" (Iraq). Isaiah 13:4-6 is highly topical. Prophecy is being fulfilled before our very eyes. Do we have any idea where this will all lead?

The Bible contains the answer, and also reveals the reason: "I will also gather all nations, and will bring them down into the valley of Jehoshaphat, and will plead with them there for my people and for my heritage Israel, whom they have scattered among the nations, and parted my land" (Joel 3:2). The nations do not realize that they already are on God's path of judgment and are being led to the greatest catastrophe in history. Events prophesied for the last days already can be seen on the horizon: "all the people of the earth be gathered against it" (Jerusalem) (Zechariah 12:3 and 14:2). We also read: "And it shall come to pass in that day, that I will seek to destroy all the nations that come against Jerusalem" (Zechariah 12:9).

We are approaching midnight, the darkest hour of world history. That is why we want to sound the warning, "Behold, the bridegroom cometh!" all the more clearly.

The return of Jesus for His Bride will not be a day

of sorrow, but one of gladness and rejoicing: "Let us be glad and rejoice, and give honour to him: for the marriage of the Lamb is come" (Revelation 19:7). The Apostle Paul instructs us to give "thanks unto the Father, which hath made us meet to be partakers of the inheritance of the saints in light" (Colossians 1:12).

For this reason we want to be prepared and clothed in fine linen: "To her was granted that she should be arrayed in fine linen, clean and white: for the fine linen is the righteousness of saints" (Revelation 19:8). We have to "put off the old man with his deeds" (Colossians 3:9) and put on the Lord Jesus Christ (Romans 13:14). Our deeds should be righteous in our marriages, in our families, in our contact with others, and in our testimonies.

As the Lord Jesus addressed this parable to His disciples (Matthew 24:3ff), let us ask ourselves further:

Who do the Disciples Represent?

The Lord Jesus warned His disciples to, "Watch therefore, for ye know neither the day nor the hour wherein the Son of man cometh" (Matthew 25:13). I believe the disciples have to be seen in the context of the Olivet Discourse, which describes the condition of the Jewish people directly before the reign of Jesus Christ can be established.

At this point, the disciples did not represent the Church, and therefore did not represent the Bride of the returning Bridegroom. Rather, they represented the virgins (i.e. wedding guests), from out of the Jewish people. That point is clear from Matthew 9:14-15, "Then came to him the disciples of John, saying, Why do we and the Pharisees fast oft, but thy disciples fast not? And Jesus said unto them, Can the children of the bridechamber mourn, as long as the bridegroom is with them? But the days will come, when the bridegroom shall be taken from them, and then shall they fast." The Lord didn't describe the disciples as the Bride, but as wedding guests because He was speaking about Israel, not the Church. Later, the apostles laid the foundation for the Church, but in this passage they still symbolize the Jewish people in the last times. They found themselves on the border between the Old and the New Covenant.

The Disciples Represent the Wedding Guests

"Then shall the kingdom of heaven be likened unto ten virgins, which took their lamps, and went forth to meet the bridegroom...And at midnight there was a cry made, Behold, the bridegroom cometh; go ye out to meet him" (Matthew 25:1, 6). Amos 5:2-4 contains an interesting parallel to the ten virgins: "The virgin of Israel is fallen; she shall no more rise: she is forsaken upon her land; there is none to raise her up. For thus saith the Lord GOD; The city that went out by a thousand shall leave an hundred, and that which went forth by an hundred shall leave ten, to the house of Israel. For thus saith the LORD unto the house of Israel, Seek ye me, and ye shall live." It is as though God used the prophet to speak symbolically about Israel in the last days, in which there remains only "ten virgins," of which only five are wise. We are concerned with the judgment upon the Jewish people at the return of Jesus in glory for the establishment of the Messianic kingdom. The 10 virgins in Jesus' parable represent Israel at the end of the Great Tribulation, at midnight, and the time of the Lord's Second Coming. This describes division in the Jewish people and judgment upon Israel. On the other hand (Matthew 25:31ff), we are concerned with the division between the nations and the judgment upon them in the parable of the sheep and the goats.

The invitation to come to the Marriage Supper will be extended to Israel after the Church has been united with Jesus and is in heaven. The Song of Solomon contains a wonderful illustration of this: "Behold his bed, which is Solomon's; threescore valiant men are about it, of the valiant of Israel. They all hold swords, being expert in war: every man hath his sword upon his thigh because of fear in the night. King Solomon made himself a chariot of the wood of Lebanon. He made the pillars thereof of silver, the bottom thereof of gold, the covering of it of purple, the midst thereof being paved with love, for the daughters of Jerusalem. Go forth, O ye daughters of Zion, and behold king Solomon with the crown wherewith his mother crowned him in the day of his espousals, and in the day of the gladness of his heart...Behold, thou art fair, my love; behold, thou art fair; thou hast doves' eyes within thy locks: thy hair is as a flock of goats, that appear from mount Gilead"

(Song of Solomon 3:7-11 and 4:1). Here, the following is described for us:

• Solomon is a picture of Jesus Christ, the returning King and Bridegroom, to take possession of His throne in Jerusalem and to present the Bride-Church.

• The valiant men around him are the armies that follow Him (Revelation 19:14).

• This all takes place at night (midnight).

• The daughters of Zion, who are told to come, are a picture of the virgins who should meet the Lord.

• The day of the marriage is described, that He has come to the Marriage Supper.

• Then the beauty of the Bride (Church), whom He presents to His people, is described.

The expectation of the Messiah will greatly increase in Israel during the time of Jacob's Trouble (Great Tribulation). One hundred and forty-four thousand Jews will be sealed (Revelation 7:4-8). The two witnesses (Revelation 11:3ff) and the "faithful and wise servants (Matthew 24:45-51) will cry out, "Behold, the bridegroom cometh." Many will come to believe and to know, on the grounds of God's Word, that the Messiah's return will be imminent. They will find instruction in God's Word.

Today the Messianic Jews in Israel are already contributing to this cry at midnight. Their churches published an encouraging challenge in the largest Israeli newspaper on the 54th Day of Independence of the state of Israel. The end of that challenge stated:

The Messianic-Jewish believers believe concerning the prophecy of the Old and New Testaments that Jesus, the Son of David, is the Messiah of our righteousness and redemption. When He appeared for the first time 2,000 years ago, He accomplished our personal redemption through the sacrifice of His blood, which atones for sin. When He appears for the second time, in the near future, He will bring the promised national redemption of our people.

Not all Jewish people will allow themselves to be prepared for the day of redemption. Just as there is a wise and faithful servant and an evil servant, there are also wise and foolish virgins. The Lord showed what is necessary where the latter is concerned: oil, a picture of the indwelling Holy Spirit (compare Psalm 45:8 and 89:21).

The "Wise" and "Foolish" Virgins

The wise virgins will allow themselves to be completely renewed by the Holy Spirit during the Great Tribulation. They will follow the Lord in complete obedience, allow themselves to be led by the Word of truth, and will not tolerate defilement. A picture of this is the 144,000 sealed Jews, of whom we read, "These are they which were not defiled with women: for they are virgins. These are they which follow the Lamb withersoever he goeth. These were redeemed from among men, being the firstfruits unto God and to the Lamb. And in their mouth was found no guile: for they are without fault before the throne of God" (Revelation 14:4-5).

William MacDonald wrote:

124

> They are called 'virgins,' those who 'were not defiled by women.' They kept their distance from the terrible idolatry and immorality of their time, and followed the 'Lamb' in unconditional obedience and devotion. Pentecost says, 'They are the "first-fruits for God and the Lamb," i.e. they are the first harvest of the time of tribulation, who enter into the millennium of peace, to then populate the earth.' They did not receive the lie of the Antichrist that man should worship a mere man. They were 'fault-less' where their consistent testimony for Christ was concerned. [5]

On the other hand, the foolish virgins are waiting for the Bridegroom, but they have not allowed themselves to be renewed. On the contrary, they have also been deceived by a lie. We notice that from their obvious connection with the "merchants": "And the foolish said unto the wise, Give us of your oil; for our lamps are gone out. But the wise answered, saying, Not so; lest there be not enough for us and you: but go ye rather to them that sell, and buy for yourselves. And while they went to buy, the bridegroom came; and they that were ready went in with him to the marriage: and the door was shut" (Matthew 25:8-10). The journey to the merchants had been fateful for the foolish virgins, for the text does not tell us that they returned with oil or with light.

Who Are the "Merchants"?

The book of Zechariah ends with this strange sentence: "In that day there shall be no more the Canaanite in the house of the LORD of hosts" (Zechariah 14:21). The New International Version uses the word "Canaanite" to translate the word "merchant." Apparently, the word "Canaanite" was a derogatory term for a merchant.

During biblical times, merchants symbolized cheating, cunning and deception. God used the prophet Hosea to write: "He [Israel] is a merchant, the balances of deceit are in his hand: he loveth to oppress" (Hosea 12:7). And Matthew the evangelist reported, "And Jesus went into the temple of God, and cast out all them that sold and bought in the temple, and overthrew the tables of the moneychangers, and the seats of them that sold doves" (Matthew 21:12). We see how close deception and sanctuary are to one another.

Many deceivers will crawl out of the woodwork in the last days and deceive many: "For there shall arise false Christs, and false prophets, and shall shew great signs and wonders; insomuch that, if it were possible, they shall deceive the very elect" (Matthew 24:24). They will "trade" with the name of Jesus. Therefore, the Lord warns, "Wherefore if they shall say unto you, Behold, he is in the desert; go not forth: behold, he is in the secret chambers; believe it not" (verse 26).

I can only imagine that the foolish virgins will be a picture of those people in Israel who fall victim to such deceivers in the last times. These people will speak of Christ (verse 23), but they will not give true light. They will make a profit with religious words, but will not lead people to rebirth.

The foolish virgins have the inspired Word of God (2 Corinthians 4:4 and Psalm 119:105), but they were not born again by the Holy Spirit. They have lamps, but no oil in their vessels.

True redemption is more than a mere confession of faith; it demands a true renewal through the Holy Spirit.

Exclusion from the Kingdom

Matthew 25:11-12 reveals that the door was shut. The other virgins came, saying, "Lord, Lord, open to us. But he answered and said, Verily I say unto you, I know you not."

We cannot obtain the "oil of the Spirit" by performing religious works, but only from Jesus. Not all of the Jewish people will be able to enter the blessing of the Messianic kingdom: "And when the king came in to see the guests, he saw there a man which had not on a wedding garment: and he saith unto him, Friend, how camest thou in hither not having a wedding garment? And he was speechless. Then said the king to the servants, Bind him hand and foot, and take him away, and cast him into outer darkness; there shall be weeping and gnashing of teeth" (Matthew 22:11-13). We learn from Ezekiel 20:37-38 that a division will occur in the people of Israel: "And I will cause you to pass under the rod, and I will bring you into the bond of the covenant: and I will purge out from among you the rebels, and them that transgress against me: I will bring them forth out of the country where they sojourn [Matthew 24:31], and they shall not enter into the land of Israel: and ye shall know that I am the LORD."

The false prophets, false christs and deceivers (i.e., merchants) mentioned in Matthew 24:5:11 and 24-26), will be purged. They will speak of Christ, but they will not have Him. They will say, "Lord, Lord" and perform many signs and wonders, but He will tell them that He does not know them (compare Matthew 7:15-23). The same thing is said to the foolish virgins (Matthew 25:12). The judgment of God will come upon the false prophets: "And mine hand shall be upon the prophets that see vanity, and that divine lies: they shall not be in the assembly of my people, neither shall they be written in the writing of the house of Israel, neither shall they enter into the land of Israel; and ye shall know that I am the Lord GOD" (Ezekiel 13:9). The Lord will deny knowing them.

The Lord will divide the sheep: "Therefore will I save my flock, and they shall no more be a prey: and I will judge between cattle and cattle. And I will set up one shepherd over them, and he shall feed them, even my servant David; he shall be their shepherd" (Ezekiel 34:22-23).

A Warning That Must Not Be Ignored

The worst thing we could do is to take note of all this and deceive ourselves by thinking that this only applies to Israel. The parable of the 10 virgins is also a warning to New Testament believers. No one who

has not been born again by the Holy Spirit will participate in the Rapture. Even today there are people who:

• Have fallen prey to the deception of mere religious knowledge.

• Belong to a church but are not born again.

• Say, "Lord, Lord" but do not belong to Him.

• Call themselves "Christians" but are not one
with Christ.

There have always been people who have led lives
different from the rest, but outward religiosity and separation from the spirit of the times are not enough. In
other words, we do not need to be worldly-minded to
be on the wrong track. A man without the Holy Spirit
is dead (Ephesians 2:1 and Romans 8:9) regardless of
his efforts and good works. The Lord Jesus told
Nicodemus, "Verily, verily, I say unto thee, Except a
man be born again, he cannot see the kingdom of
God...That which is born of the flesh is flesh; and that
which is born of the Spirit is spirit. Marvel not that I
said unto thee, Ye must be born again" (John 3:3; 6-7).

The Decisive Criteria

It doesn't matter how much or how little we know
Jesus and strive to follow Him. What counts is whether
He knows us. To the foolish virgins who stood before
the closed door, He said, "Verily I say unto you, I know
you not" (Matthew 25:12).

It is not enough for you to know the Lord Jesus
Christ from hearsay, by visiting a church, from reading
books or from other Christians. You must have a per-

sonal meeting with Him in order for Him to know you. This only takes place through surrender and rebirth, through genuine conversion, by accepting His invitation.

The Difference

Regarding the 10 virgins, the Bible says, "Five of them were wise, and five were foolish" (Matthew 25:2). Although they all looked the same on the outside, and were waiting for the Bridegroom, the Lord Jesus did not have a personal relationship with the five foolish virgins, and said to them: "I know you not" (verse 12).

What does it mean to be "foolish" in God's eyes? Matthew 7:26 answers: "Every one that heareth these sayings of mine, and doeth them not, shall be likened unto a foolish man, which built his house upon the sand." Whoever hears the Word of God but does not act upon it with all his heart is not truly converted, does not obediently follow Jesus, and does not live his life for Him, is foolish.

The Bride of the Lord Jesus is compared to a virgin whose purity the Apostle Paul strove for, "For I am jealous over you with godly jealousy: for I have espoused you to one husband, that I may present you as a chaste virgin to Christ" (2 Corinthians 11:2). We read about such virgins in Revelation 14:4-5, and learn that the Lamb has bought them; they follow Him, they are virgins, they are without guilt and they are without fault.

Five of the virgins proved to be foolish because they did not take any oil with them (Matthew 25:3). Oil is a picture of the Holy Spirit and of a life with God. Those who are religious but without God in their lives cannot meet Him; their lamps will burn out one day.

The five other virgins prove wise in that they take "oil in their vessels with their lamps" (verse 4). Their lamps burn constantly from the supply of oil. This means they live for God.

Before a Word Comes Over Our Lips...

...the Lord already knows what we want to say. He "knoweth the thoughts of man" (Psalm 94:11). Of the Son of God we read, [Jesus] "knowing their thoughts said..." (Matthew 9:4). So it is not surprising that the Lord would classify the 10 virgins before their condition had been revealed: "Five of them were wise, and five were foolish" (Matthew 25:2). But this also means that Jesus knows our condition, and so we must seek help in Him in time. We should not deceive ourselves, but pray in time for a complete renewal.

The concluding admonition, "Watch therefore, for ye know neither the day nor the hour wherein the Son of man cometh" (Matthew 25:13), is addressed to all of us. For the foolish it is a call to be converted, and for the wise it is a call to consistency. "For God hath not appointed us to wrath, but to obtain salvation by our Lord Jesus Christ, who died for us, that, whether we wake or sleep, we should live together with him" (1 Thessalonians 5:9-10).

Only Jesus can give us the gift of the Holy Spirit. The foolish virgins expected the wise virgins to replenish their oil supply when they had run out. These could not give them any (Matthew 25:8-9). We cannot give our redemption to anyone else. Charles H. Spurgeon said, "Grace does not flow in our veins (through our relatives)."

Everyone has to receive for himself the gift of the Holy Spirit; each one has to come to Jesus himself. "For God so loved the world, that He gave His only begotten Son, that whosoever believeth in him should not perish, but have everlasting life" (John 3:16). "In whom ye also trusted, after that ye heard the word of truth, the gospel of your salvation: in whom also after that ye believed, ye were sealed with that holy Spirit of promise, which is the earnest of our inheritance until the redemption of the purchased possession, unto the praise of his glory" (Ephesians 1:13-14).

1. *Hannoversche Allgemeine Zeitung,* 4.12.02
2. *Hannoversche Allgemeine Zeitung,* 4.12.02
3. *Zurcher Oberlander,* 4.16.02
4. *Schweizerzeit,* 1.11.02
5. *Commentary on the New Testament* by William McDonald

Chapter 9

THREE PERIODS OF CHURCH HISTORY

Although I believe Matthew 25 (see chapter 8) is primarily
addressed to Israel, it can certainly apply spiritually to the
Church of Jesus Christ.

Period One: The Apostolic and Post-Apostolic Time (from Pentecost to the beginning of the 3rd century after Christ)

It was the time when Jesus Christ was the "first love," characterized by the daily, living expectation of His return, which the Lord describes as follows: "Then shall the kingdom of heaven be likened unto ten virgins, which took their lamps, and went forth to meet the bridegroom" (Matthew 25:1).

The Word was so alive and effective among the believers at the time of the apostles and in early Church history that they awaited the Lord's return continually. They greeted one another with the word, *"Maranatha,"* which means, "Our Lord is coming."

It was an evangelistic movement that was focused on the Lord and went towards Him with burning torches. In almost all of their letters, the apostles wrote about the living hope of Jesus' return, and they spoke about it to the churches as something that could take place at any moment. For instance, the Apostle Paul rejoiced when writing to the church at Thessalonica: "For they themselves shew of us what manner of entering in we had unto you, and how ye turned to God from idols to serve the living and true God; and to wait for his Son from heaven, whom he raised from the dead, even Jesus, which delivered us from the wrath to come" (1 Thessalonians 1:9-10). And to Timothy, he wrote, "Henceforth there is laid up for me a crown of righteousness, which the Lord, the righteous judge, shall give me at the day; and not

134

to me only, but unto all them also that love his appearing" (2 Timothy 4:8).

The return of the Lord Jesus is mentioned almost 300 times in the 270 chapters of the New Testament. A German Bible commentary explains:

> We shall only be able to attain to the spiritual heights of New Testament sanctified lives when the expectation of the Lord in our faith-lives has as much room as it did in the churches of the apostolic time. Professor Kaftan says, 'The wonderful power of the first Christian churches was founded solely on the living hope of the visible, personally returning Christ.' [1]

Exactly how much of the apostolic time was filled with waiting for Jesus to return is illustrated by the statement of the Apostle Peter, which corresponds to the parable of the 10 virgins. Peter remembered Jesus speaking about this, and probably had this in mind when he wrote: "We have also a more sure word of prophecy; whereunto ye do well that ye take heed, as unto a light that shineth in a dark place, until the day dawn, and the day star arise in your hearts" (2 Peter 1:19). The virgins went to meet their Lord with their lamps burning, which points to the prophetic Word, which must be placed on a lampstand. The Lord demands, "Let your loins be girded about, and your lights burning; and ye yourselves like unto men that wait for their lord, when he will return from the wedding; that when he cometh and knocketh, they may open unto him immediately" (Luke 12:35-37). The first Church Age was indeed very much characterized by the expectation of the Lord, as Jesus said in His parable: "Then shall the kingdom of heaven be likened unto ten virgins, which took their lamps, and went forth to meet the bridegroom."

Period Two: Loss of First Love and Spiritual Sleep

The first love for the Lord Jesus and His Word was soon lost. Thus the expectation of His return also declined. This period is described in Matthew 25:5 as follows: "While the bridegroom tarried, they all slumbered and slept."

In the letter to the church at Ephesus, the Lord had John write: "Nevertheless I have somewhat against thee, because thou hast left thy first love. Remember therefore from whence thou art fallen, and repent, and do the first works; or else I will come unto thee quickly, and will remove thy candlestick out of his place, except thou repent" (Revelation 2:4-5).

Soon after the apostles had died, the light of the expectation of Jesus' return started to burn out in the churches. There was a lot of activity, but no longer was there a living expectation of the first love of a bride who is waiting for her bridegroom. This expectation had gone to sleep.

The lamps of the wise virgins, which announced the coming of the bridegroom, had continued to burn. They did what Jesus required of them. They let their lights burn, and they waited for Him. They heeded the prophetic Word "like a light that burneth in a dark place until the day dawns and the day star rises in your hearts."

Viewed from this perspective, I believe the Lord wanted to say to the church at Ephesus, "You are no longer like a virgin or a bride who is going to meet her bridegroom with her lamp burning. You have lost your first love, although you have the light of the prophetic Word. What use is it to you, however, if you do not use it to come towards Me? So repent, or I will take the lamp of the prophetic Word away from you."

And that is just what happened. The light of the prophetic Word was almost lost in the following centuries: "While the bridegroom tarried, they all slumbered and slept." Church history developed just as it is described here. The Lord Jesus tarried; He did not return. Consequently, Christianity was overcome by a spiritual sleep that made all expectation of His return slumber. The watchfulness that the Lord Jesus had continually told them of had decreased. Because He knew of this, He called to His disciples, "Let your loins be girded about, and your lights burning...And ye yourselves like unto men that wait for their lord, when he will return from the wedding; that when he cometh and knocketh, they may open unto him immediately" (Luke 12:35-36). "Watch ye therefore: for ye know not when the master of the house cometh, at even, or at midnight, or at the cockcrowing, or in the morning: lest coming suddenly he find you sleeping" (Mark 13:35-36).

Along with the declining hope of Jesus' return, the knowledge of Christ's return quickly disappeared. It is shocking that almost no mention of His return has been made in Christian literature since about 300 A.D. We find almost no texts concerning the expectation of His return for His Bride (i.e. the Rapture of His Church) in any commentary or hymn from around 300 A.D. to the 18th century. There was hardly any mention of the Rapture of the Church, even during the Reformation. There was a wonderful return to the truth of the Scriptures and to the topic of His return at the end of time (i.e. the Day of Judgment), but everything else concerning His return disappeared under a "veil" in Christianity.

Gerhard Herbst wrote:

> In churches and free churches, also in hymns, there is no difference between the Rapture and the return of Jesus in glory. Where the return of Christ is mentioned at all, this generally refers to the visible return of Christ on the Mount of Olives. This, however, is Israel's expectation, and not that of the Church of Jesus Christ...The Rapture of the Church is the next event that the Church can expect. It is not attached to any spectacular sign. [2]

Period Three: Spiritual Awakening

This third period is between 150 and 200 years old. It coincides with the return of the first Jewish immigrants to their homeland.

This third phase of church history lies at the end of the time of grace, and is known as the "endtimes." It is described in the parable of the 10 virgins as follows, "And at midnight there was a cry made, Behold, the bridegroom cometh; go ye out to meet him. Then all those virgins arose, and trimmed their lamps" (Matthew 25:6-7).

A mighty working of the Holy Spirit within Christianity had taken place since the beginning of the 19th century (and even earlier). Revival movements had taken place. Missionary organizations blossomed. New hymns and songs were written and the return of the Lord Jesus at the Rapture was suddenly recognized again. John Nelson Darby (1800-1882), the founder of the Plymouth Brethren, was one who preached this lost truth. He was wide-awake as far as this was concerned, and with others, he put the light of Jesus back on the lampstand. Not only in England, but also in America many people published literature emphasizing the theme of Jesus' return for His Church and newly illuminating it.

Darby believed the Church had degenerated since the days of the apostles, and he wanted to contribute to a new revival of the apostolic time. *The German Evangelical Lexicon for Theology and Church* states: "Extensive journeys to West Europe, North America and Australia served the Philadelphia Spirit-Church of the endtimes as a preparation for the return of Jesus."

In the 19th century the difference between the

"Rapture," the "Day of the Lord," and the "Judgment Seat of Christ" was discovered anew. Simultaneously, many free churches [According to *The Oxford Dictionary*, a "free church" is a Christian church that has dissented or seceded from an established church] arose because of courageous men and women who left the existing church systems.

How did the rediscovery of the Rapture occur? It was like somebody awakening from a deep sleep. Was this not a cry of the Holy Spirit of God who revived many people because we have entered the time of Jesus' return? Yes, we certainly are living at the midnight hour when the cry of the Spirit of Jesus is being heard: "Behold, the bridegroom cometh; go ye out to meet him!" (Matthew 25:6).

It is surely not by chance that almost parallel to this awakening within the Church, the beginning of Israel's restoration and the sudden awakening of the Jews to return to their homeland is taking place. Both have been produced by the Spirit of God. Our Lord is coming!

1 *Wuppertaler Studienbible*
2 Gerhard Herbst, Newsletter 4/1999

Chapter 10

SETTLING THE ACCOUNT

A certain level of tension and anxiety always accompanies an audit of any type. Questions abound: Have we done everything according to the rules? What will the balance be? Every financial detail must be recorded, and at the end of the year all of the facts are laid out on the table.

The same is true in our lives as far as our gifts and assets are concerned; all things have been recorded in heaven, and the great audit will take place at the end of time. The Lord Jesus said,

For the kingdom of heaven is as a man travelling into a far country, who called his own servants, and delivered unto them his goods. And unto one he gave five talents, to another two, and to another one; to every man according to his several ability; and straightway took his journey. Then he that had received the five talents went and traded with the same, and made them other five talents. And likewise he that had received two, he also gained other two. But he that had received one went and digged in the earth, and hid his lord's money. After a long time the lord of those servants cometh, and reckoneth with them. And so he that had received five talents came and brought other five talents, saying, Lord, thou deliveredst unto me five talents: behold, I have gained beside them five talents more. His lord said unto him, Well done, thou good and faithful servant: thou hast been faithful over a few things, I will make thee ruler over many things: enter thou into the joy of thy lord. He also that had received two talents came and said, Lord, thou deliveredst unto me two talents: behold, I have gained two other talents beside them. His lord said unto him, Well done, good and faithful servant; thou hast been faithful over a few things, I will make thee ruler over many things: enter thou into the joy of thy lord. Then he which had received the one talent came and said, Lord, I knew thee that thou art an hard man, reaping where thou hast not sown, and gathering where thou hast not strawed: and I was afraid, and went and hid thy talent in the earth: lo, there thou hast that is thine. His lord answered and said unto him, Thou wicked and slothful servant, thou knewest that I reap where I sowed not, and gather where I have not strawed: thou oughtest therefore to have put my money to the exchangers, and then at my coming I should have received mine own with usury. Take therefore the talent from him, and give it unto him which hath ten talents. For unto every one that hath shall be given, and he shall have abundance: but from him that hath not shall be taken away even that which he hath. And cast ye the unprofitable servant into outer darkness: there shall be weeping and gnashing of teeth (Matthew 25:14-30).

The Right and Wrong Use of God's Grace

The Apostle Paul could say that he had been conscientious in dealing with the grace God gave him: "By the grace of God I am what I am: and his grace which was bestowed upon me was not in vain; but I laboured more abundantly than they all: yet not I, but the grace of God which was with me" (1 Corinthians 15:10). Paul put this grace to good use.

In his second letter to the church at Corinth, the

Apostle Paul placed the responsibility on the Church as well, "We then, as workers together with him, beseech you also that ye receive not the grace of God in vain" (2 Corinthians 6:1). To receive something in vain is the worst thing we can do. Certainly it is worse than if we had never had something. The Greek word for "in vain" is *kenos*, which means "empty, hollow, useless, powerless, vain."

We are concerned in our parable with the final settlement of the account: "After a long time the lord of those servants cometh, and reckoneth with them" (Matthew 25:19). They were given the instruction, when they had received their talents, to occupy themselves until he returned (Luke 19:13). Do we remember this command from the Lord, and live our lives accordingly? The time for settling the account is coming for each of us!

The Significance for Israel

In the Olivet Discourse, Jesus admonished His disciples, "he that shall endure unto the end, the same shall be saved" (Matthew 24:13). The phrase, "unto the end" makes it clear that the Lord was not referring to the Rapture, but to the end of the Great Tribulation, its conclusion, and His return.

Thus, we should see the disciples of the Lord from a prophetic perspective as the Jewish remnant in the last days. We should not omit this context when we consider the parable of the talents. The Lord Jesus said, "For the kingdom of heaven is as a man travelling into a far country, who called his own servants, and delivered unto them his goods…After a long time the lord of those servants cometh, and reckoneth with them"(Matthew 25:14, 19). It is clear that this refers to Israel from the fact that the Lord traveled to a far country and returned to this land after a long time. So it must refer to the servants who lived in this land. It becomes apparent that we are not concerned here with the Rapture, but with the return of Jesus Christ to the land of Israel. This is where He was, and this is where He will return.

This is even clearer from Luke 19: "And as they heard these things, he added and spake a parable, because he was nigh to Jerusalem, and because they thought that the kingdom of God should immediately appear. He said therefore, A certain noble man went into a far country to receive for himself a kingdom, and to return…And it came to pass, that when he was returned, having received the kingdom, then he commanded these servants to be called unto him, to whom he had given the money, that he might know how much every man had gained by trading" (verses 11-12, 15). At that time there were Jews who believed the Kingdom of God for Israel "should immediately appear." The Messiah was there and had entered Jerusalem riding on a donkey, and they called out to Him, "Hosanna; Blessed is he that cometh in the name of the Lord: Blessed be the kingdom of our father David, that cometh in the name of the Lord: Hosanna in the highest" (Mark 11:9-10). They thought He would disperse all of Israel's enemies, particularly the Romans, and set up the promised kingdom of David. But Jesus explained to them by means of a parable that the establishment of this kingdom they awaited had been postponed.

This parable relates that Jesus was in the land of Israel 2,000 years ago, but the Jewish people rejected Him. The Lord then left the land of Israel and returned to heaven in order to establish another kingdom through His Holy Spirit: the spiritual Kingdom of the Church. He will return to the earthly land of Israel to establish the kingdom of God there after He has received this kingdom for Himself, which means the complete number of Gentiles has been reached (Romans 11:25),

Acts 15:14-17 makes this point very clear: "Simeon hath declared how God at the first did visit the Gentiles, to take out of them a people for his name [this is the Church]. And to this agree the words of the prophets; as it is written, after this I will return, and will build again the tabernacle of David, which is fallen down; and I will build again the ruins thereof, and I will set it up [Jesus returns for Israel]: that the residue of men might seek after the Lord, and all the Gentiles, upon whom my name is called, saith the Lord, who doeth all these things." All nations will come under Israel's blessing in the Millennium of Peace through the Lord Jesus.

After the Church Age, at the return of Jesus for His people, the "servants"—that is, the remnant of Israel that lived between the Rapture of the Bride– Church and the return of Jesus– will be called upon to give an account. For instance, Psalm 50:3-5 states: "Our God shall come, and shall not keep silence; a fire shall devour before him, and it shall be very tempestuous round about him. He shall call to the heavens from above, and to the earth, that he may judge his people. Gather my saints together unto me; those that have made a covenant with me by sacrifice."

The Lord will then judge His people because the Church of Jesus Christ in the present day has the task of setting up the testimony of the Gospel and putting her spiritual gifts to good use. The testimony of the Church will end, however, on the day of the Rapture. Then Israel's spiritual renewal will begin, for example, through the 144,000 Jews (Revelation 7:4-8) and the "two witnesses" of Revelation 22:3ff. Then the task will be taken over by Israel. The Great Tribulation follows Jesus' First Advent; the Church Age was inserted between the two.

Israel will be judged according to its works during this time when the Lord Jesus Christ returns. Compare in this connection Jesus' words concerning the wise and evil servants in Matthew 24:45-51.

Those who have done well with the talents entrusted to them will enter the joy of the Lord, that is, the kingdom of Christ on earth (Matthew 25:21, 23). We can also apply the words of Revelation 5:10 to these faithful ones, "And hast made us unto our God kings and priests: and we shall reign on the earth." But those who have been unfaithful will be "cast out" (will perish). That is what the words of Matthew 25:30 mean: "And cast ye the unprofitable servant into outer darkness: there shall be weeping and gnashing of teeth." This is a judgment on earth, for those who are born again and are raptured to heaven will not be cast into the outer darkness.

We must also apply this parable to us spiritually, as the Church has been given the task in this present age to be a witness for Jesus.

The Distribution of the Gifts

"And unto one he gave five talents, to another two, and to another one; to every man according to his several ability" (Matthew 25:15).

A talent was a silver coin that was the largest monetary unit at the time, weighing approximately 36 kilos. A talent was made up of about 10,000 denarii, and a denarius was the daily wage of a simple workman. A person would have to work more than 27 years without stopping to earn a talent.

Therefore, we are concerned here with large sums of money that were entrusted to the servants. The Holy Spirit does not give us small gifts. One has more, and the other less. The gifts are very different, but it is always a "large sum."

Interesting is that the talents were distributed to the recipients "according to his several ability" (Matthew 25:15). According to 1 Corinthians 12:11, we know that the Spirit of God distributes the gifts as He will,

"But all these worketh that one and the selfsame Spirit, dividing to every man severally as he will." But does the Lord regard how far we are seeking the gifts, and how willing our hearts are? First Corinthians 14:12 could be referring to this: "Even so ye, forasmuch as ye are zealous of spiritual gifts, seek that ye may excel to the edifying of the church." First Corinthians 12:31 states, "But covet earnestly the best gifts." And Ephesians 4:16 explains, "From him [Christ] the whole body fitly joined together and compacted by that which every joint supplieth, according to the effectual working in the measure of every part, maketh increase of the body unto the edifying of itself in love." The servant who only had received one talent probably never sought more. Here we see the necessity of spiritual zeal.

I believe there is a clear example of this in the Old Testament. When it came to making the robes for the High Priest, the Lord said, "And thou shalt speak unto all that are wise hearted, whom I have filled with the spirit of wisdom, that they may make Aaron's garments to consecrate him, that he may minister unto me in the priest's office" (Exodus 28:3). The Lord has filled the "wise hearted" with the spirit of wisdom. They brought a certain precondition, willingness, with them; they fulfilled God's demand beforehand.

This means much more, however, namely that the Lord also wants to use the natural gifts He has endowed us with. A person who has never played a musical instrument will not suddenly be able to play the piano when he has been born again. Or someone who has had a speech impediment will not suddenly receive the gift of preaching when he is converted.

Faithfulness is Required

It does not depend on whether we have received much (five talents) or little (one or two talents), but whether we were faithful in using our gifts. The Lord said the same thing to the one who was faithful with the five talents as He said to the one with two talents, "Well done, thou good and faithful servant: thou hast been faithful over a few things, I will make thee ruler over many things: enter thou into the joy of thy lord" (Matthew 25:21, 23). The servant who only received one talent should have proven himself faithful by putting to use this one talent, for it says, "It is required in stewards, that a man be found faithful" (1 Corinthians 4:2). But he was unfaithful, and therefore he was rebuked and judged by the Lord (Matthew 25:24ff).

In practical terms, this could mean that a faithful mother and housewife will receive a greater reward in eternity than an evangelist who hardly used his gift. Somebody who is poor can give more from what little he has than a rich man who gives from his wealth (compare Mark 12:41-44). In many circumstances, a handicapped person can do more than a healthy person.

We do not necessarily need to be young to be fishers of men (Matthew 4:19), or to have eyes that see. The Lord can use old people and blind people who are dedicated to Him.

There once was a 70-year old blind woman who loved her French Bible. She asked a missionary to underline John 3:16 in red. The missionary was surprised by the woman's request, but he obliged nonetheless. Somehow she managed to sit down on a bench in front of a school. When the children came out, she asked them if they had paid attention in their French lesson. They all said they had. Then she asked the children, one after another, to read to her the underlined text (in French), and asked them if they had understood it. When they said they hadn't, she told them the Gospel of Jesus Christ, beginning with this text. Later on it was learned that 24 men had become preachers of the Gospel as a result of this blind woman's ministry. All of them had testified that this ministry, which was carried out in great physical weakness, had been relevant for their lives. This blind Christian woman did not complain about her "fate," but because her heart burned for the lost, she prayed that the Lord would use her. He gave her this idea of the red underlined Bible verse, and she put it into practice. She was faithful with the little she had received. Certainly she heard the words from the mouth of the Lord: "Well done, thou good and faithful servant: thou has been faithful over a few things, I will make thee ruler over many things: enter thou into the joy of thy Lord." Will the Lord Jesus receive you one day with these words?

Chapter **11**

ISRAEL FROM GOD'S PERSPECTIVE

Feelings and opinions regarding Israel can range from curiosity to unfathomable hatred. But the most important question to consider is this: How does God see the Jewish people?

" Then shall the King say unto them on his right hand, Come, ye blessed of my Father, inherit the kingdom prepared for you from the foundation of the world: for I was an hungred, and ye gave me meat: I was thirsty, and ye gave me drink: I was a stranger, and ye took me in: Naked, and ye clothed me: I was sick, and ye visited me: I was in prison, and ye came unto me. Then shall the righteous answer him, saying, Lord, when saw we thee an hungred, and fed thee? Or thirsty, and gave thee drink? When saw we thee a stranger, and took thee in? or naked, and clothed thee? Or when saw we thee sick, or in prison, and came unto thee? And the King shall answer and say unto them, Verily I say unto you, Inasmuch as ye have done it unto one of the least of these my brethren, ye have done it unto me" (Matthew 25:34-40).

Today, politicians and the media portray the Jewish people in a one-sided and negative way. Even the pastors of some churches publicly announce their dislike of Israel. But such attitudes serve to promote an even more distorted picture of Israel.

Somebody once asked how the Holocaust was even possible. The answer is that the German people had severed their relationship with God, and therefore allowed themselves to fall prey to Nazi propaganda.

How the nations view Israel is insignificant. What matters is God's regard for Israel. Ultimately, He will prove to be right in His verdict upon His covenant people, and not without grave consequences for the nations.

Of course, not everything the Jews do is good. In fact, the majority of Jews have no relationship with God. All the stages in Israel's history have been characterized by sin. Yet God has always kept His promises. Even when Israel reached rock bottom and rejected the Messiah, the Lord said,"Ye shall not see me henceforth, till ye shall say, Blessed is he that cometh in the name of the Lord" (Matthew 23:39). Jesus' words are a clear indication that He has not rejected His people, but that they have an endtime destiny of restoration.

Israel Remains the Focus of Prophecy

Matthew 25 emphasizes that as a nation Israel is important to God, and that His covenant with this people endures throughout history. The nations will gather before the Lord of glory and be judged according to how they treated the Jews. The focus will still be on Israel when Jesus returns.

Israel has retained its national identity for all of these years—a remarkable testimony to the topical nature of God's Word. If Israel had no further significance, it would have disappeared from spiritual history a long time ago. If the Church had taken over all the blessings that belong to Israel, there would be no more judgment at the end of time. Here, however, a clear distinction is made between the nations on one hand, and the least of Jesus' brethren on the other. "When the Son of man shall come in his glory, and all the holy angels with him, then shall he sit upon the throne of his glory: and before him shall be gathered all nations: and he shall separate them one from another, as a shepherd divideth his sheep from the goats…And the King shall answer and say unto them, Verily I say unto you, Inasmuch as ye have done it unto one of the least of these my brethren, ye have done it unto me" (Matthew 25:31-32, 40).

Who are Jesus' brethren? The Jews who will be persecuted during the Great Tribulation and will come to believe in Jesus, as well as all the others who came to believe in Him. In Matthew 28:10, we read, "Then said Jesus unto them, Be not afraid: go tell my brethren that they go into Galilee, and there shall they see me." Hebrews 2:16-17 says, "For verily he took not on him the nature of angels; but he took on him the seed of Abraham. Wherefore in all things it behoved him to be made like unto his brethren, that he might be a merciful and faithful high priest in things pertaining to God, to make reconciliation for the sins of the people." And Psalm 122:5-8 says, "For there [in Jerusalem] are set thrones of judgment, the thrones of the house of David. Pray for the peace of Jerusalem: they shall prosper that love thee. Peace be within thy walls, and prosperity within thy palaces. For my brethren and companions' sakes, I will now say, Peace be within thee."

I find Jesus' use of the words "my brethren" very moving, because the phrase clearly expresses how God really sees the Jewish people. The Lord came from these people, and that is why He identifies

Himself so strongly with His fellow countrymen.

Israel is Important to Jesus

God told Abraham, "I will bless them that bless thee, and curse him that curseth thee: and in thee shall all families of the earth be blessed" (Genesis 12:3). What was the reason for such serious words? The blessing for all nations was to come from Israel, i.e. from the descendants of Abraham. Jesus Christ is this blessing. If the blessing for all nations comes from Abraham's descendants, then it is not surprising that the curse will come upon all those from among the nations that curse Israel.

This is why Jesus has to return to Jerusalem and reign there as king, because Jerusalem was chosen for Him forever. "For David said, The LORD God of Israel hath given rest unto his people, that they may dwell in Jerusalem for ever" (1 Chronicles 23:25). When the Queen of Sheba visited King Solomon, she uttered the prophetic words, "Blessed be the LORD thy God, which delighted in thee to set thee on his throne, to be king for the LORD thy God: because thy God loved Israel, to establish them for ever, therefore made he thee king over them, to do judgment and justice" (2 Chronicles 9:8).

Werner Penkazki made the following comments on Genesis 12:3:

> "These words of God are like a key to under-
> standing history. I see historical events, their
> cause and effect, in connection with these words.

> Blessing and curse upon people and nations are connected with their attitude to the people of God...The coming dramatic events concerning Israel are the culmination of the history of God with the world under the aspect of this blessing or curse" (*Israel, the Third World War and Us*, p.9f — not available in English).

Ultimately, this promise of blessing and cursing will be fulfilled in Jesus' judgment upon the nations, for here the terms "blessing" and "curse" also occur. To the one He says, "Then shall the King say unto them on his right hand, Come, ye blessed of my Father, inherit the kingdom prepared for you from the foundation of the world" (Matthew 25:34). The divine verdict upon the others, however, was, "Then shall he say also unto them on the left hand, Depart from me, ye cursed, into everlasting fire, prepared for the devil and his angels" (Matthew 25:41).

Israel's Place in the Bible

Almost every book of the Old Testament includes prophecies concerning Israel and its future. Among them we find unfulfilled prophecies such as the reign of the Messianic kingdom.

• The Old Testament book of Genesis contains 50 chapters. Eleven of these chapters deal with the creation of heaven and earth, the creation of man, the Fall of man, the Flood, the building of the tower of Babel and the development and spread of the nations. This is a relatively small space for such great themes. The other 39 chapters deal with Israel's history, beginning with Abraham, Isaac and Jacob.

• The "Israel" theme is continued in New Testament prophecy, where the way to the Messianic kingdom and to all eternity is described (see Matthew 23:39, chapters 24 and 25, Acts 15:14-17, Romans 9-11 and the book of Revelation).

For instance, we read in Acts 3:19-21, "Repent ye therefore, and be converted, that your sins may be blotted out, when the times of refreshing shall come from the presence of the Lord; and he shall send Jesus Christ, which before was preached unto you: whom the heaven must receive until the times of restitution of all things, which God hath spoken by the mouth of all his holy prophets since the world began."

The people of Israel did not repent at that time, but the time will come when this will take place. Then the Lord will return from heaven and fulfill all the remaining prophecies (Daniel 7:13ff; 9:24; 12:1-3; and Zechariah 12:10-14).

God Identifies with Israel

Matthew 25:40, 45 states, "And the King shall answer and say unto them, Verily I say unto you, Inasmuch as ye have done it unto one of the least of these my brethren, ye have done it unto me...Then shall he answer them, saying, Verily I say unto you, Inasmuch as ye did it not to one of the least of these, ye did it not to me."

When Assyrian King Sennacherib wanted to attack

the kingdom of Judah and capture Jerusalem during the time of Hezekiah, God said: "Whom hast thou reproached and blasphemed? And against whom hast thou exalted thy voice, and lifted up thine eyes on high? Even against the Holy One of Israel" (2 Kings 19:22).

God made it clear through the prophet Zechariah that Israel was the apple of His eye: "he that toucheth you toucheth the apple of his eye" (Zechariah 2:8).

When the king of the Canaanites and his captain, Sisera, attacked Israel, the Lord gave Israel victory over him through Deborah, Barak and Jael. Then Deborah and Barak sang: "Praise ye the LORD for the avenging of Israel, when the people willingly offered themselves...My heart is toward the governors of Israel, that offered themselves willingly among the people. Bless ye the LORD...Curse ye Meroz, said the angel of the LORD, curse ye bitterly the inhabitants thereof; because they came not to the help of the LORD, to the help of the LORD against the mighty" (Judges 5:2, 9, 23).

If only the nations knew whom they were opposing when they defame Israel!

Israel's Incomparability to the Nations

God separated Israel from the other nations for eternity. The Jews have always held a prominent place before all other nations, and they will so forever.

• The nation's borders are determined by the num-

160

ber of the sons of Israel (Deuteronomy 32:8).

• Jerusalem is the geographical center of all the nations that surround her (Ezekiel 5:5).

• Israel is the center of the earth (Ezekiel 38:12).

• "And what one nation in the earth is like thy people Israel, whom God went to redeem to be his own people, to make thee a name of greatness and terribleness...For thy people Israel didst thou make thine own people for ever; and thou, LORD, becamest their God. There now, LORD, let the thing that thou hast spoken concerning thy servant and concerning his house be established for ever, and do as thou hast said. Let it even be established, that thy name may be magnified for ever, saying, The LORD of hosts is the God of Israel, even a God to Israel: and let the house of David thy servant be established before thee" (1 Chronicles 17:21-24, compare also with 16:14-17).

These words contain deep truths. Israel is incomparable to the other nations through God's sovereign election. Israel serves His glory. This fact remains true for eternity. The name of the Lord will be exalted forever because He will not let go of His people.

The hatred from God's enemies, however, is directed against this. Werner Penkazki wrote of this:

> The roots of the Holocaust go deep, and from the very beginning of the nation of Israel attempts were made to exterminate her (by Egypt). To be God's chosen people also means suffering, besides the knowledge of the Most High and the experience of His blessing. A world that hates God,

also despises His people, of course. God is not
tangible, so they attack His people (Psalm 83:1-4).[1]

The fact that the above-mentioned truths remain,
that they have retained their validity up to the present
day, is proven in that the judgment of God will come
upon the nations when Jesus returns.

But what are the godless nations in comparison to
Israel? Here, too, the Bible gives us an answer:

• The Word of God will remain when all the voices
against Israel have been silenced, "The grass with-
ereth, the flower fadeth: but the word of our God
shall stand for ever" (Isaiah 40:8).

• Jesus will return to redeem His people: "Behold,
the Lord GOD will come with strong hand, and his
arm shall rule for him: behold, his reward is with
him, and his work before him. He shall feed his flock
like a shepherd: he shall gather the lambs with his
arm, and carry them in his bosom, and shall gently
lead those that are with young" (Isaiah 40:10-11).

• Then the nations are described: "Behold, the
nations are as a drop of a bucket, and are counted as
the small dust of the balance: behold, he taketh up the
isles as a very little thing...All nations before him are
as nothing; and they are counted to him less than
nothing, and vanity. To whom then will ye liken God?
Or what likeness will ye compare unto him?" (Isaiah
40:15, 17-18, compare also with Psalm 62:9-10).

My dear reader, can't the One who "taketh up the
isles as a very little thing" also solve your problems?

Our Attitude Toward Israel Counts

From what perspective do we judge Israel? Do we see God's covenant people from the Bible's perspective, or do we judge it on a purely emotional level, according to the mistakes Israel has made, or based on the viewpoint of the media?

It is not a coincidence that the Church of Jesus Christ is alive at this time. We too have a task to fulfill as far as the Jewish people are concerned. The generations before us have failed. We must be careful to not repeat history.

Esther was queen at the Persian court for one reason: To raise her voice in the distress of the Jewish people. Mordecai sent a message to Esther, "Think not with thyself that thou shalt escape in the king's house, more than all the Jews. For if thou altogether holdest thy peace at this time, then shall there enlargement and deliverance arise to the Jews from another place; but thou and thy father's house shall be destroyed: and who knoweth whether thou art come to the kingdom for such a time as this?" (Esther 4:13-14). Esther had to take a stand. God would help the Jewish people with or without her help, but her silence would have cost her a great blessing.

God *will* help the Jewish people. They have been chosen by Him for eternity and are not destined to fall. Therein lies the honor and glory of Jesus Christ in the proof of the reliability of His Word. But He wants to do it through us. And that is why we must not remain silent.

1 *Werner Penkazki, Israel, der dritte Weltkrieg und wir*

Chapter 12

GOD'S CRITERIA FOR JUDGMENT UPON THE NATIONS

How should Christians behave toward the Jewish people? Does it even matter? In this chapter we will see why it is important what a person or a whole nation thinks about Israel.

" Then he shall say also unto them on the left hand, Depart from me, ye cursed, into everlasting fire, prepared for the devil and his angels: for I was an hungered, and ye gave me no meat: I was thirsty, and ye gave me no drink: I was a stranger, and ye took me not in: naked, and ye clothed me not: sick, and in prison, and ye visited me not. Then shall they also answer him, saying, Lord, when saw we thee an hungered, or athirst, or a stranger, or naked, or sick, or in prison, and did not minister unto thee? Then shall he answer them, saying, Verily I say unto you, Inasmuch as ye did it not to one of the least of these, ye did it not to me. And these shall go away into everlasting punishment: but the righteous into life eternal" (Matthew 25:41-46).

God makes it clear through the prophet Isaiah there is no interruption in history as far as Israel's election is concerned: "For Zion's sake will I not hold my peace, and for Jerusalem's sake I will not rest, until the righteousness thereof go forth as brightness, and the salvation thereof as a lamp that burneth. And the Gentiles shall see thy righteousness, and all kings thy glory: and thou shalt be called by a new name, which the mouth of the LORD shall name" (Isaiah 62:1-2).

God will not be silent where Jerusalem is concerned, even beyond the Church Age, until righteousness goes forth in the return of His Son. And in this very judgment upon the nations at the return of the Lord in power and glory, the full validity of these words will be recognizable. Let us look back seven decades when Nazism arose in Germany. As a result, more and more Jews were alienated until a general boycott was proclaimed in 1933 when one man stood in his pulpit and cried, "Whoever does not cry out for the Jews cannot praise God!"

On November 9th 1938, when in the so-called Nazi Reich 1,300 synagogues were set fire to and destroyed, innumerable Jewish houses, apartments and stores demolished, 100 Jews murdered and tens of thousands sent to concentration camps, this man stood up and publicly proclaimed: "Western history is irrevocably connected with the people of Israel, according to the will of God...an expulsion of the Jews from the Western World will mean an expulsion of Christ, for Jesus Christ was a Jew...if the synagogues are burning today, tomorrow it will be the churches." And that is exactly what happened.

This man had underlined Psalm 74:8-10 in his Bible, "They said in their hearts, Let us destroy them together: they have burned up all the synagogues of God in the land. We see not our signs: there is no more any prophet: neither is there among us any that knoweth how long. O God, how long shall the adversary reproach? Shall the enemy blaspheme thy name for ever?" He wrote the date, 11.9.38 next to these verses.

Dietrich Bonhoeffer dared to publicly stand up for the Jewish people and condemned the National Socialist regime. We may not agree with him on all theological issues, but he openly confessed to his belief in the "endtime return of the people of Israel to Christ and their spiritual path." This attitude cost him his life. He was thrown into prison and killed by the Nazis shortly before the end of the war. While he was in prison, he wrote a famous German hymn. A doctor in the concentration camp named Buchenwald testified, "This man doubtless had a living relationship with God. I have never seen a man pray like that..."

In 1940, Bonhoeffer wrote, "The Church confesses to having seen the deliberate use of brute force, the physical and psychological suffering of innumerable innocent people, oppression, hatred and murder, without having raised her voice in protest, without finding ways to help them. She has become guilty of the murder of the weakest and most defenseless brothers of Jesus Christ."

A time will come that will be similar to the Holocaust, but much worse and more violent. A man like Hitler will arise, but his actions will be even more brutal. The Bible calls him the "Antichrist." In the Revelation of Jesus Christ we find the program for the endtimes. In the 12th chapter, we read how the "dragon" will pursue the woman who has given birth to a child (Judaism, from which came Jesus Christ), and how he will try at all costs to destroy the Jews through the Antichrist and his regime. In the darkest time of the Jewish people (which is ahead of them), everything will depend upon how the people living at that time will have behaved towards Israel.

I believe it is decisive how Christians behave towards the Jews. Do we join forces with this world and accept everything the media writes about Israel? Or are we on Israel's side because God the Father and God the Son—the Jew, Jesus Christ—are on Israel's side? Throughout the last 2,000 years of history, since the birth of Christ, it has proven true that whoever touches Israel touches the apple of God's eye (compare Zechariah 2:12).

The King Will Come Again

Jesus' Discourse on the Mount of Olives speaks primarily about the Jewish people who are living in their own land again in the endtimes, and will have to go through the Great Tribulation before the return of Christ. The Lord's words make clear the position of the Jews in God's eyes, even if the whole world is crying out against them in protest today.

In chapters 40-47, the prophet Ezekiel wrote that the temple would be rebuilt in Jerusalem. Jesus will return after the Tribulation, and will seat Himself on the throne of glory: "When the Son of man shall come in his glory, and all the holy angels with him, then shall he sit upon the throne of his glory" (Matthew 25:31). His throne will stand in the middle of Jerusalem for 1,000 years. We may conclude from God's Word that angels and the Church will accompany the Lord Jesus at His return (Jude 14; 1 Thessalonians 3:13 and Zechariah 14:5).

The glory of the eternal God was present in

Solomon's temple during Old Testament times. God made this promise concerning the Messiah: "Yet have I set my king upon my holy hill of Zion" (Psalm 2:6). The people from out of the nations who have survived the Great Tribulation will have to appear before Him and be judged according to the good or evil that they did to the Jews: "And before him shall be gathered all nations: and he shall separate them one from another, as a shepherd divideth his sheep from the goats" (Matthew 25:32). There will be three groups among those who will be judged: the brethren, the sheep and the goats. The "brethren" are the Messianic-believing Jews and other believers, the "sheep" are the saved, and the "goats" are the unsaved from out of all nations.

The Lord will judge the "goats" according to what they should have done, but did not do. It does not seem irrelevant to me that their sins of omission are six-fold: 1)"Ye gave me no meat"; 2)"Ye gave me no drink" (Matthew 25:42); 3)"Ye took me not in"; 4)"Ye clothed me not"; 5)"Ye visited me not" (verse 43); 6)"Inasmuch as ye did it not to one of the least of these, ye did it not to me"(verse 45).

The Lord will praise the "sheep" for their seven-fold deeds: 1)"Ye gave me meat"; 2)"Ye gave me drink"; 3) "Ye took me in" (Matthew 25:35); 4) "Ye clothed me"; 5)"Ye visited me"; 6)"Ye came unto me"; 7)"Inasmuch as ye have done it unto one of the least of these my brethren, ye have done it unto me" (verse 40).

The Verdict upon the Sheep

Matthew 25:33-40 says, "And he shall set the sheep on his right hand, but the goats on the left. Then shall the King say unto them on his right hand, Come, ye blessed of my Father, inherit the kingdom prepared for you from the foundation of the world: for I was an hungred, and ye gave me meat: I was thirsty, and ye gave me drink: I was a stranger, and ye took me in: Naked, and ye clothed me: I was sick, and ye visited me: I was in prison, and ye came unto me. Then shall the righteous answer him, saying, Lord, when saw we thee an hungred, and fed thee? Or thirsty, and gave thee drink? When saw we thee a stranger, and took thee in? or naked, and clothed thee? Or when saw we thee sick, or in prison, and came unto thee? And the King shall answer and say unto them, Verily I say unto you, Inasmuch as ye have done it unto one of the least of these my brethren, ye have done it unto me."

What is the measure for the verdict upon the righteous?

1. Their treatment of Jesus: What counts is what people did or did not do to the Lord. Every sin is against God. Joseph offers a striking example of this when he was in Egypt and Potiphar's wife tried to seduce him. He said to her, "How then can I do this great wickedness, and sin against God?"(Genesis 39:9). When we lie to people, or harm them in any way, we are actually doing it to God first, which makes the matter so grave. This is why our relation-

171

ship to Jesus is so important.

A person's standing before the Lord is apparent in the way he or she treats his or her fellow Christians. Our behavior reflects our faith. Those who come to faith in Jesus Christ during the Great Tribulation will do good to their brothers, and consequently to Jesus. Their deeds will be the fruit of their faith. We see this from the fact that the kingdom was prepared for them from the foundation of the world: "Then shall the King say unto them on his right hand, Come, ye blessed of my Father, inherit the kingdom prepared for you from the foundation of the world" (Matthew 25:34).

They not only visited Jesus, but came to Him: "I was in prison, and ye came unto me" (verse 36). There is a difference between visiting Jesus and really coming to Him, as illustrated in whether we pretend to be Christians or really know Jesus.

The "goats" on His left were completely surprised when they heard that they had not served Him. They had lived under a fatal delusion, "Then shall they also answer him, saying, Lord, when saw we thee an hungred, or athirst, or a stranger, or naked, or sick, or in prison, and did not minister unto thee?"(verse 44). Even in Jeremiah's time, the Lord said of those who thought they were serving Him, "The priests said not, Where is the LORD? And they that handle the law knew me not" (Jeremiah 2:8, compare also with John 16:2-3 and Matthew 7:21-23).

Christians must be on Israel's side, for the Spirit of

God who lives in the born-again Christian is the same Spirit who restored Israel, and He cannot contradict Himself.

When a person is against Israel, another spirit is at work in him, which is why Jesus makes the direct connection between Israel and Himself. What we do or do not do to His brothers, we do or fail to do to Him.

2. Their behavior towards the brothers: Isaiah 54:17 says, "No weapon that is formed against thee shall prosper; and every tongue that shall rise against thee in judgment thou shalt condemn. This is the heritage of the servants of the LORD, and their righteousness is of me, saith the LORD." And Proverbs 27:18 says, "Whoso keepeth the fig tree shall eat the fruit thereof."

In the Revelation of Jesus Christ, we find a reference to the help that many people will give Israel during its persecution in the Great Tribulation: "And when the dragon saw that he was cast unto the earth, he persecuted the woman which brought forth the man child...And the earth helped the woman, and the earth opened her mouth, and swallowed up the flood which the dragon cast out of his mouth" (Revelation 12:13, 16). We will not discuss here the issue of whether Israel will, in fact, find refuge in Petra (Edom) during the Great Tribulation, as many Bible exegetes believe. The earth is the realm of the rule of man. There will be men on the earth who will help and protect the persecuted Jews. The reward for this love that comes from faith in Jesus will be admittance into the Messianic kingdom and eternal life. They belong as sheep on the pasture of the Good Shepherd: "Then shall the King say unto them on his right hand, Come, ye blessed of my Father, inherit the kingdom prepared for you from the foundation of the world...And these shall go away...into life eternal" (verses 34 & 46, compare also with Proverbs 19:7; Matthew 10:40; 2 Timothy 1:16 and Hebrews 10:34).

The Old Testament contains a wonderful illustration of this: "And it came to pass, when David was come to Mahanaim [when he was fleeing from Absalom], that Shobi the son of Nahash of Rabbah of the children of Ammon, and Machir the son of Ammiel of Lodebar, and Barzillai the Gileadite of Rogelim, brought beds, and basons, and earthen vessels, and wheat, and barley, and flour, and parched corn, and beans, and lentiles, and parched pulse, and honey, and butter, and sheep, and cheese of kine, for David, and for the people that were with him, to eat: for they said, The people is hungry, and weary, and thirsty, in the wilderness" (2 Samuel 17:27-29). When Barzillai finally crossed the Jordan with King David, we read, "Now Barzillai was a very aged man, even fourscore years old: and he had provided the king of sustenance while he lay at Mahanaim...And the king said unto Barzillai, Come thou over with me, and I will feed thee with me in Jerusalem" (chapter 19:32-33).

The Verdict upon the Goats

Matthew 25:41-46 explains: "Then shall he say also unto them on the left hand, Depart from me, ye cursed, into everlasting fire, prepared for the devil and his angels: for I was an hungred, and ye gave me no meat: I was thirsty, and ye gave me no drink: I was a stranger, and ye took me not in: naked, and ye clothed me not: sick, and in prison, and ye visited me not. Then shall they also answer him, saying, Lord, when saw we thee an hungred, or athirst, or a stranger, or naked, or sick, or in prison, and did not minister unto thee? Then shall he answer them, saying, Verily I say unto you, Inasmuch as ye did it not to one of the least of these, ye did it not to me. And these shall go away into everlasting punishment: but the righteous into life eternal."

The righteous God judges the "goats" according to the same criteria as the "sheep" (James 2:13). The "goats" despised Jesus, and therefore His brothers did as well. They did not believe in Jesus, and did not help His people. Instead, they allowed themselves to become integrated in the program of the Antichrist; they persecuted, denounced and drove the Jews and believers to their deaths.

In His reproach, Jesus did not only say that they did not visit Him, but He left out the words, "Ye came not unto Me." This means that they did not have a genuine relationship with Him.

A report during the Nazi era read: "On six days in the week the new elite worked in the concentration camps. On Sundays they rested and went with their wives and children to church, and after church..."[1] In spite of all their religiosity, the Nazis hated God and His people. They spoke against the Lord, and therewith against His people. We read the lament in Psalm 44:22, "Yea, for thy sake are we killed all the day long; we are counted as sheep for the slaughter." Jude 14-15 states: "And Enoch also, the seventh from Adam, prophesied of these, saying, Behold, the Lord cometh with ten thousands of his saints. To execute judgment upon all, and to convince all that are ungodly among them of all their ungodly deeds which they have ungodly committed, and of all their hard speeches which ungodly sinners have spoken against him." And Psalm 83:2-5 says, "For, lo, thine enemies make a tumult: and they that hate thee have lifted up the head. They have taken crafty counsel against thy people, and consulted against thy hidden ones. They have said, Come, and let us cut them off from being a nation: that the name of Israel may be no more in remembrance. For they have consulted together with one consent: they are confederate against thee."

Such people will be excluded from the kingdom and will be eternally lost, which is actually the fate prepared only for the devil and his angels: "Then shall he say also unto them on the left hand, Depart from me, ye cursed, into everlasting fire, prepared for the devil and his angels" (Matthew 25:41, compare also with verse 46 and Revelation 20:10, 15). These people thought they were so clever, but in the end it was revealed that they were no more than people who had been deceived by the devil (Revelation 20:8-10).

Yes, there is a place called hell, even though many people find this idea so hard to bear. Not everyone will go to heaven, because eternal punishment and eternal life are both described with the fateful word "eternal." If the one were not eternal, the other would not be eternal either.

Christianity's Relationship to Israel Reveals its Relationship to Christ

How is it possible that Christian churches and institutions can be against Israel? Is it because they do not have a relationship with Jesus Christ and are representatives of a nominal Christianity? They judge everything with their sin-tainted understanding, but the Word of God is the truth, and not a humanistic concept of righteousness.

The Jews have been branded, persecuted, pursued, excluded from society, forcibly baptized, held responsible for catastrophes, and murdered all because of a false understanding of Scripture. And it was not noticed that catastrophes came because the Jews were treated in this way. These people made themselves God's enemies.

• Regarding the mass murder of Jews, the "Stuttgart Confession of Guilt" of the Evangelical Church in Germany of 1948, says, "Because Israel crucified the Messiah, she rejected her rejection and destiny."[2] Is this one of the reasons for the empty churches today?

• What spirit drove Rick Godwin, a leading charismatic in the US, to say, "What Israel? — the Church…this is God's Israel and not the stinking one on the other side of the Mediterranean."[3]

Cursing and Blessing Through People's Dealings with Israel

The following are a few examples from history:

• The fate of the greatest empires was determined by their attitude towards Israel: Egypt under the Pharaohs (Exodus 14:23-28), Assyria under King Sennacherib (2 Kings 19:35-37), Babylon (Isaiah 47:6 onwards & Daniel 5:23 onwards), Rome (70 A.D.), Spain in the 16th century, Russia in the 19th century under the Czars, Great Britain in the 20th century and Nazi Germany at the time of the Holocaust.

• In the US anti-Judaism was followed in 1929 by the great collapse of the banks, the world economic crisis and mass unemployment.

• A quotation from the book, *From Eternity to Eternity,* clarifies the above examples:

> God's chosen people, Israel or the Jews are also called the 'apple of God's eye,' and those who touch them will inevitably bring the judgment of God upon themselves. Europe had to experience the pain of this, and states, empires and dynasties that had existed for centuries fell in less than two generations. The common characteristic of these fallen empires was 'anti-Judaism': in Spain in the

16th century, in the rest of Europe in the 19th and 20th century. Anti-Semitism was prevalent in Russia, then in France and Poland. In Germany the discrimination and persecution culminated in a planned genocide...England, who took in the Jews, and fought against the devilish regime in Germany, betrayed the Israelis in Palestine when they wanted to establish their own state, by delivering heavy arms to the Arabs...this was simultaneously judgment upon the British empire, whose downfall could no longer be prevented. Europe, a small continent that ruled the world, sank within a few decades into political insignificance. On the other side, the rise of the U.S. began, leading to the present sole world power.[4]

• Somebody once said, "The harassing of the Jews was followed by the first world war — the persecution of the Jews was followed by the second world war — the worldwide hatred of the Jews will be followed by the third world war."

• In 1215 the Roman Catholic Church decided at her Lateran council that all Jews in her territory had to wear a "yellow patch." As a result, the lands within the sphere of influence of the Catholic Church became impoverished. Why did the Catholic clergy issue this order? For the same reason the Lord Jesus gave concerning the scribes and the Pharisees: "They shall put you out of the synagogues: yea, the time cometh, that whosoever killeth you will think that he doeth God service. And these things will they do unto you, because they have not known the Father, nor me" (John 16:2-3).

• During the Crusades the Jews were locked in the synagogues, which were then set on fire. The Crusades ended in 1291 with the Muslims victorious over the "Christians."

• After Martin Luther published his pamphlet, "Concerning the Jews and Their Lies," in 1543, the Reformation, which until then had spread like wildfire in Europe, lost half of its range of influence. The great counter-Reformation took place only two years after this pamphlet was published.

• Spain lost its sea-power in 1588 when it banned all the Jews from its country, and appropriated its possessions in the 16th century.

• "Anti-Judaism" began to spread in Russia in 1878. The Russian Orthodox Church and the Czars ordered numerous "pogroms" (aimed at the persecution and destruction of the Jews). The result was the October Revolution, the rise of communism and the death of the Czar family. Churches were also closed.

• The granaries of the world became impoverished under communism because of the denial and persecution of Christians and Jews.

• The battle of Stalingrad was lost exactly one year to the day after the "Wannsee Conference" (in Berlin) where the extermination of the Jews was decided. This defeat became the greatest and most torturous defeat for the German army.

• The Third Reich lasted for 12 years (1933 -

1945). It seems that God wanted to hold up the number 12 — the number of the tribes of Israel — before the eyes of the world.

• Germany sank into ruins and was divided by a wall. The Germans had imprisoned the Jews in walled ghettos.

• The reparation payments that Germany had to make to Israel under Konrad Adenauer from 1952 brought Germany the economic miracle.

• East Germany did not pay a cent, and became an impoverished territory.

• Since 1973, when the political opinion in Europe turned against Israel again the German "economic miracle" had slowly subsided. In its place, problems like the oil crisis, recession and high unemployment figures rose.

• In 1989, the East German government decided to grant right of abode to Russian Jews. Shortly afterwards, the wall in Berlin fell without any bloodshed. The wall came with Arab-Semitism and it disappeared with friendship to the Jews.[5]

• When Laban persecuted his son-in-law Jacob (Israel), and was rightly angry with him because Jacob had deceived him and left without telling him, God met Laban. He said to the man, "Take heed that thou speak not to Jacob either good or bad"(Genesis 31:24). When it came to a discussion between Jacob and Laban, the latter said, "It is in the power of my hand to do you hurt: but the God of your father spake unto me yesternight, saying, Take thou heed that thou speak not to Jacob either good or bad" (verse 29). Notice Laban did not call God "*his*" God, but "the God of *your* father."

On one hand, Laban was forbidden to touch Jacob (i.e. Israel). On the other hand, he knew that the Lord had blessed him on account of Jacob. "And Laban said unto him, I pray thee, if I have found favour in thine eyes, tarry: for I have learned by experience that the LORD hath blessed me for thy sake" (Genesis 30:27).

• When the Egyptian Pharaoh ordered the midwives to kill all the Israelites' newborn sons, they refused to obey him. And what happened? "Therefore God dealt well with the midwives: and the people multiplied, and waxed very mighty. And it came to pass, because the midwives feared God, that he made them houses" (Exodus 1:20-21).

• The Lord pronounced the following curses upon Ammon and Moab, "An Ammonite or Moabite shall not enter into the congregation of the LORD; even to their tenth generation shall they not enter into the congregation of the LORD for ever: because they met you not with bread and with water in the way, when ye came forth out of Egypt; and because they hired against thee Balaam the son of Beor of Pethor of Mesopotamia, to curse thee" (Deuteronomy 23:3-4).

• In contrast, the Lord said of Edom and Egypt, "Thou shalt not abhor an Edomite; for he is thy brother: thou shalt not abhor an Egyptian; because thou wast a stranger in his land" (Deuteronomy

23:7).

• On one hand, the Bible speaks about a future judgment upon Egypt (Isaiah 19:1 onwards and Zechariah 14:18-19). God probably has to punish Egypt because it oppressed, deceived and persecuted Israel, and will do so in the future. On the other hand, the Bible speaks in the same chapter of the book of Isaiah about a future blessing in Egypt, and about its salvation (Isaiah 19:19 onwards) — presumably because the Egyptians took in Joseph, because the Jewish people as a nation were born there, and because later on they also took in the Lord Jesus. Here the blessing of Jacob is probably fulfilled. The Pharaoh of that time said to Joseph, "The land of Egypt is before thee; in the best of the land make thy father and brethren to dwell; in the land of Goshen let them dwell...And Joseph brought in Jacob his father, and set him before Pharaoh...And Jacob blessed Pharaoh, and went out from before Pharaoh" (Genesis 47:6-7 & 10).

Can a Christian Tread Down His Own Roots?

The Jews have been imprisoned for 2,000 years. Shouldn't we have stayed with Israel, especially those who believe in Jesus as Messiah? Jesus said, "I was in prison, and ye came unto me" (Matthew 25:36).

Many people have not visited the "least of Jesus' brethren" in their "prison." Deceived by the "god of this world," they have even joined the ranks of those who are against Israel. They have robbed Israel of her biblical promises, imprisoned the Jews and isolated them because many Christians have never come to Jesus themselves to stay with Him. He said, "And these shall go away into everlasting punishment: but the righteous into life eternal" (Matthew 25:46).

The Church's roots are steeped in Judaism (Romans 11:17 onwards). It owes its existence to it, for the Jewish people brought us Christ. There would be no Church if there were no Israel. It was God's plan to create Judaism in order to build the Church from it. The Lord Jesus did not say without reason, "Salvation is of the Jews" in John 4:22, "of whom as concerning the flesh Christ came" (Romans 9:5). When Christians are against Israel, they are treading down their own roots. Let us, therefore, who are from the roots of Israel's patriarchs take the words of Romans 11:18 to heart: "Boast not against the branches. But if thou boast, thou bearest not the root, but the root thee" (see also Romans 15:27).

1 Ramon Bennet, *Wenn Tag und Nacht Vergehen*
2 Werner Penkazki, *Israel, der dritte Welkrieg und wir*
3 Dave Hunt, *Jerusalem, Spielball der Volker*
4 Gian Luca Carigiet, *Von Ewigkeit zu Ewigkeit*
5 Werner Penkazki, *Israel, der dritte Weltkrieg und wir*

Chapter 13

THE WORLD SITUATION BEFORE THE RETURN OF JESUS

"Throughout the history of man known to us, there has never been a time in which the signs of the times have been closer and taking place in quicker succession than today. Our world is changing." [1]

Biblical historian Edmund Jacob wrote, "The Bible speaks with such urgency of the intervention of God in history, and how He is realising His plan with Israel, that we should make sure that we take heed of the signs which point to His plan."[2]

The following quote regarding Hebrews 10:19-25 ("but exhorting one another: and so much the more, as ye see the day approaching") appeared in the Christian publication entitled *Factum*:

"The reference to the approaching day of the return of Christ shows us the urgency of this text. When should this verse be applied, if not today?"[3]

Author Rainer Wagner wrote:

> We cannot regard the proclaimed signs of the end times separated from our present day. This would be an unspiritual relativism of that which Jesus said in Matthew 16:2-3...Much of that which is printed in the newspapers can be explained by the prophetic Word of the Bible...However this may be, they [the signs of His coming] show that the world is ripe for judgment![4]

The following statements are not for "spoiled" Christians who, in keeping with a feel-good Christianity, want to continue being spoiled, nor are they intended for those who are only looking for edification.

As the signs of the endtimes are given by God Himself, however, we do well to concern ourselves with them, for they proclaim the greatest event in the history of mankind: the glorious return of the Son of God.

The edification lies therein that we may know that these signs do not proclaim the end of the world, but a completely new era under the lordship of Jesus Christ.

Unbelievers are warned, but Christians are encouraged to spread the Gospel, to watch and to pray, to inwardly prepare and say, "Come quickly, Lord Jesus!"

Most of the signs of the Great Tribulation concern Israel and the return of Jesus in glory. These signs and the readiness for the Rapture have gained topical relevance since the Jewish people have returned to Israel. Signs have their precedents, which can be seen and also heard more today than ever before.

Swiss Bible teacher Dr. Roger Liebi mentioned 12 signs from the Olivet Discourse at a meeting in Bavaria that I would like to mention and elaborate upon.

Deception

"Jesus answered and said unto them, Take heed that no man deceive you. For many shall come in my name, saying, I am Christ; and shall deceive many" (Matthew 24:4-5).

"And many false prophets shall rise, and shall deceive many" (Matthew 24:11).

"For there shall arise false Christs, and false prophets, and shall shew great signs and wonders; insomuch that, if it were possible, they shall deceive the very elect" (Matthew 24:24).

The waves of deception have become noticeably greater since the 20th century:

• Various waves of the charismatic movement were mentioned.

• False prophethood, in that revivals were spoken

about that did not occur.

• Signs of healing were described as being of more significance than sanctification. Hundreds of healing miracles were spoken about, but not one can be medically proven.

• The Toronto Blessing crept into 50,000 churches around the globe and deceived many. Some people exposed to this fraud behaved like animals.

• Many have been and many will be deceived by the increase of Eastern religious teachings and their gurus. The esoteric wave and the New Age movement have drawn millions under its spell.

• Many orthodox Jews in Israel acclaimed Lubavitcher Rabbi Menachem Mendel Schneerson, who died in 1994, as the Messiah (see Chapter 1).

"But evil men and seducers shall wax worse and worse, deceiving, and being deceived" (2 Timothy 3:13).

Wars and Rumors of Wars

"And ye shall hear of wars and rumours of wars: see that ye be not troubled: for all these things must come to pass, but the end is not yet. For nation shall rise against nation, and kingdom against kingdom" (Matthew 24:6-7).

• The return of the Jews to the land of their fathers has been characterized by two world wars. These wars were unprecedented in history. World War I prepared a land for a people. World War II prepared a people for a land. These wars did not signify the end, for they led to the founding of the state of Israel, and therefore had to take place.

World War I resulted in the deaths of 14 million people; chemical weapons of mass destruction were used for the first time. Approximately 55 million people were killed in World War II, where atomic weapons were used for the first time. In the end, Germany was at war with 60 countries.

• Numerous national conflicts and civil wars, particularly the fall of the Iron Curtain, have resulted from World Wars I and II. The increase of civil wars is said to be estimated at 100 percent since the end of the East/West conflict. We have mourned the deaths of 50 million people since the end of World War II, who had been victims of countless conflicts between the nations.

Just think about the situation of the world since the war in Iraq, the Middle East conflict, the Kurdish problem, Afghanistan, the Kashmir conflict, Chechnya, Africa (Sudan, etc.), North Korea, Latin America, and the squabbles in former Yugoslavia. Approximately 50 war-like conflicts are taking place right now.

According to the World Health Organization, 50,000 people in the refugee camp in Dafour (Sudan) perished in the summer months alone. The Society for Threatened Peoples has even placed the death toll at 120,000 [Exact information is not available]. More than one million people are said to be fleeing in Western Sudan; approximately 500,000 have died before reaching the death camps.[5]

American publisher Norman Podhoretz remarked: "The fourth world war has begun (the third was the cold war between East and West). We are confronted by terrorists who are tired of life, who could reach us in our homeland with nuclear, chemical or biological weapons, without our having any appropriate defense. Therefore Islamic terrorism is the greatest threat."[6]

Journalist Tom Schimmeck of Hamburg wrote: "The world has become a vast battlefield; terrorism is everywhere; it will remain and even increase...we need new world politics."[7]

Modern means of communication have made it possible to hear and see via satellite the conflicts being fought around the globe. This is in keeping with the words of Jesus, "Ye shall hear of wars and rumours of wars." We see, read and hear about war propaganda and wars to an almost unbearable degree.

The 20th century is referred to as being a century with a death toll of 190 million people as a result of wars and persecution.

It has been stated that 400,000 scientists are engaged in inventing new weapons and improving existing ones.

UNICEF has reported that governments today spend more money in four days for arms purposes than they spend annually on helping their neighbors. UNICEF's annual budget is $75 million dollars, the production of a submarine costs $125 million US dollars.

Famines

"And there shall be famines...in divers places" (Matthew 24:7).

The 20th century has been described as being the century of famines. Today an estimated 800 million

190

people are starving.[8]

Nearly 500 million people are threatened with starvation; over 200 million of them are children. It is estimated that 30 people die each minute of starvation. Sixty percent of all Africans had less to eat than what the UNO considers a daily minimum for survival.

A million children die monthly worldwide through hunger, disease and violence.[9]

Pestilence

"There shall be...pestilences...in divers places" (Matthew 24:7).

Many scientists speak about a return of the plagues. According to a report from the World Health Organization, tuberculosis and malaria are gaining ground with "unprecedented aggression." Cholera and yellow fever are appearing in regions that were previously regarded as safe. In addition to this, completely new infectious diseases are appearing on the scene."[10]

At least 50 million people have been infected with the AIDS virus, and already 16 million people have died as a result.

Nearly 5 million people in 2003 alone were infected with HIV – more than in any year before. UNAIDS, the AIDS prevention program of the United Nations, has reported that the number of infected increased from about 35 million in 2001 to about 38 million by the end of 2003.

Every six seconds a person becomes infected with the

AIDS virus—that is almost 16,000 people each day. Half of the newly infected are between the ages of 25 and 34 years old.

New epidemics in East Europe have claimed the lives of 60 percent of the world's population. Around 1.3 million people are already infected there. There were 160,000 in 1995.

Scientists are concerned. The pharmacological industry has not been able to develop a vaccine nor a cure, and nothing is in sight.

Reinhard Kurth, virologist and head of the Robert Koch Institute, laments, "AIDS is the greatest medical catastrophe of modern times, only comparable with the plague."[11] Isn't this statement relevant, particularly where Matthew 24:7 is concerned: "There shall be famines, and pestilences, and earthquakes."

In Germany alone there are at least 800,000 people who have been infected with hepatitis.

Drug addiction, which also costs more and more people their lives, is also worth mentioning. For every heroin addict there are about 15 people who have an addiction to alcohol.

Allergies have reached an almost incalculable and hardly explicable degree.

The increasing number of skin cancers is said to be caused by environmental changes and the hole in the ozone layer.

More and more people are suffering from depression. Psychologists and psychotherapists are having a field day.

According to a United Nations estimate, up to 30 percent of the world's population are affected by some form of psychiatric problems. Valium is prescribed 5 million times a month in the USA.

Earthquakes

"There shall be...earthquakes in divers places" (Matthew 24:7).

Although earthquakes have always existed, the frequency and the number of its victims have risen rapidly. Seismographs register worldwide 150 perceptible and one million measurable tremors in the earth's crust annually, with increasing tendency.

A scientific hypothesis says that the number of earthquakes doubles every decade.[12]

Others believe that there aren't necessarily more earthquakes, but we are hearing about them more than ever before. The reason for this is the number of seismological institutes that have better equipment. In 1931 there were 350 seismographs and today we have more than 4,000.

The modern seismological records make another interesting phenomenon visible; namely, a "wavelike" occurrence. The worldwide seismic activity shows an increase and a decline. Geologist Steven A. Austin commented, "It looks rather like birth pains. When will a new global increase of earthquakes be?"[13]

It is noteworthy that the Lord Jesus said concerning the signs of the endtimes, "All these are the beginning of sorrows" (NIV translates this as "birth pains") (Matthew 24:8).

Troubles

"For nation shall rise against nation, and kingdom against kingdom; and there shall be earthquakes in divers places, and there shall be famines and *troubles*: these are the beginnings of sorrows" [birth pains] (Mark 13:8).

• The last century, as also in our day, has been characterized by revolutions, uprisings and riots. Think about the October Revolution in Russia (1917) and the cultural revolution in China (1965-1969), which had worldwide results for innumerable people. Then there was the Islamic revolution in Persia (1979), later that under Ayatollah Khomeini, then the revolution of the terror organizations up to the present day, with increasingly horrific results.

• A growing perplexity in governments is also perceptible. The roaring of the sea of nations and its waves is becoming stronger and fear of the future is increasing (compare Luke 21:25-26). "Since the end of the Cold War the sea of the nations has never been as turbulent as in our day."[14] Somebody made the following statement:

> Our day is making it apparent that humanity has come to the end of the line. In the economic sphere we have reached the limits of growth. In human medicine we stand before insoluble problems, in spite of all our research. Art and culture demonstrate chaos since the happenings of the 1960's. We have reached a collapse where ecological damage is concerned. In the employment of atomic energy many fear the worst

case scenario. In politics the immense perplexity is spreading.[15]

German Bible translator Hans Bruns wrote : Everyone who has eyes to see can see that there is chaos in the world, one great mess of confusion and opposition, a great rift down the middle of everything."

Hans Christian Knuth, bishop of the Evangelical Lutheran Church in Germany, compared the earth with the sinking of the Titanic:"The upper classes are still dancing in the ballrooms whilst the first are already dying."[16]

French politician Valery Giscard d'Estaing declared, "The world is unhappy because she does not know where she is going, and because she has a feeling that if she knew, she would find that she was going to her downfall."

Persecution

"Then they shall deliver you up to be afflicted, and shall kill you: and ye shall be hated of all nations for my name's sake" (Matthew 24:9).

Although this refers to the Great Tribulation, and the beginning of the birth pains, this also has its forerunners. The greatest number of Christian martyrs is not to be found at the time of the first Christians, but in the 20th century; these were killed above all under communism and Islam. Statistics for 2002 report 200,000 murdered Christians.

Judaism has always been hated for one single reason: Jesus. This is very clear from Psalm 83:2-4, "For, lo, thine enemies make a tumult: and they that hate thee have lifted up the head. They have taken crafty counsel against thy people, and consulted against thy hidden ones. They have said, Come, and let us cut them off from being a nation; that the name of Israel may be no more in remembrance."

Apostasy

"Then shall many be offended [NIV translates this as "turn away from the faith"], and shall betray one another, and shall hate one another" (Matthew 24:10).

This also refers to the Great Tribulation when a tremendous division will take place among the Jewish people. Some of them will make a covenant with the Antichrist, while others will recognize the Messiah.

But our time is also characterized by apostasy, beginning visibly with the so-called Age of Enlightenment, from the "glorious" discovery of evolution and later through communists who had the impudence to say that the first Christians had been communists ("they had all things common," Acts 4:32). Since the student revolutions of the 1960s, many of them departed from their Christian faith, adhered to other religions and ideologies and total sexual liberality was achieved.

And today? Most churches are becoming emptier and emptier, the number of people leaving them is increasing and the churches are being sold. People are distancing themselves from the Bible and its guidelines. Sociology has taken the place of biblical religious instruction in schools. Ordained ministers no longer believe in the virgin birth, the physical resurrection of Jesus Christ, and certainly not in His return.

Simultaneously sinful movements are increasing. Liberal theologians reject all the foundations of Christianity and every fact of spiritual history. They are deceived deceivers or, according to the words of Jesus, "blind leaders of the blind" (Matthew 15:14). Faith in the Word of God is being systematically and deliberately destroyed.

The homosexual movements are being received into the Church while the "fundamentalists" are being cast out.

Female "theologian" Elga Sorge published the "new" ten commandments in which it says among other things, "You may commit adultery; you can't help it." Ms. Sorge calls herself a "goddess." The terms "goddess," "Jesa Christa," and the "spiritess" are also used in feminist theology.

Antichristian movements are increasing more and more. One report stated:

> Those who seek information about 'witches' on the Internet are immediately presented with a million web-sites. The cult of witchcraft is thriving...occultism is enjoying increasing popularity. The esoteric section in bookstores is many times the size of those on the Christian faith. [17]

All this is preparing the way for the Antichrist, the greatest deceiver of all times. But 2 Thessalonians 2:3 instructs, "Let no man deceive you by any means: for that day shall not come, except there come a falling away first, and that man of sin be revealed, the son of perdition."

Our time is characterized by moral degeneration, super-stition and material greed, and is already contaminated by the spirit of the Antichrist. The apostasy of today will reach its climax and culminate in the appearing of the Antichrist. Second Thessalonians 2:8-10 says, "Then shall that Wicked [NIV translates this as "lawless one"]...Even him, whose coming is after the working of Satan with all power and signs and lying wonders, and with all deceivableness of unrighteousness in them that perish; because they received not the love of the truth, that they might be saved."

Terrorism

"And fearful sights and great signs shall there be from heaven" (Luke 21:11).

The NIV translates the Greek words for "fearful sights" as "fearful events." The Amplified Bible writes of "sights of terror." The words come from the terms "fear," "terror," "terrorize," and "put fear into."

Michael Drosnin wrote that the root of the word "terrorism" has a very significant meaning:

> In the Talmud and in the Midrash this very term occurs together with the end of the days and describes the time before the appearing of the Messiah. Simultaneously the expression refers to the moment in the history of Israel in which the efforts to obtain peace...are coupled with terrorist attacks. Perhaps these are the birth pains at the end of the days? [18]

Jeremiah 14:19 also speaks about the same thing, "We looked for peace, and there is no good; and for the time of healing, and behold trouble!" What is the international terrorism other than a means to terrorize people? More security measures have to be taken in the 21st century to prevent terrorist attacks than ever before.

It is interesting that the Hebrew word for an act of violence is *hamas*. And this act of violence is closely connected with the people and land of Israel. We read these words in Isaiah 60:18 concerning the millennium of peace, "Violence shall no more be heard in thy land, wasting nor destruction within thy borders; but thou shalt call thy walls Salvation, and thy gates Praise."

London-based Islamic newspaper *Asharq al-Awsat* (London) contained this comment after the hostage drama in Beslan: "The painful truth: all the terrorists in the world are Muslims."[19]

Dr. Roger Liebi describes the four main phases of Islamic terrorism as follows:

1. Since 1920 it has been directed against the first Jewish settlers and the English occupying powers.

2. After 1948 a more intensive phase of terrorism against the Jewish state began.

3. Since 1967 an even more intensive phase is visible. This not least of all through Yasser Arafat, his Fatah organization, the PLO, and others. Aircraft and ships have been hijacked.

4. Since 2001 Islamic terrorism has entered into an even more extreme phase. The destruction of as many people as possible is its aim, not only in Israel but worldwide.

Mankind has been in a state of unrest and terror since the "signs of heaven" on September 11, 2001 when terrorists flew two airplanes into the World Trade Center in New York. Even these things will come to an end, however, just as the prophet Isaiah says in Isaiah 17:14, "In the evening, sudden terror! Before the morning, they are gone" (NIV). The time before evening and morning is the night; this is being introduced by greater worldwide terror. The Church of Jesus Christ does not belong to the night of the Great Tribulation, however, which is why we may assume that she will be raptured beforehand. The Bible says in this connection, "Ye are all the children of light, and the children of the day: we are not of the night, nor of darkness" (1 Thessalonians 5:5). The increasing terror through terrorism could sooner or later lead to an alliance of Western states and lead them to call for a strong man. Journalist Tom Schimmeck, whom I have already quoted, writes this concerning terrorism: "What is lacking is the better plan, the new world politics with a genuine multilateral strategy, to combat terrorism. It will take a lot of time and perhaps more terror to bring it into being. The United Nations need a new, strong authority for this."[20]

We could look upon the hole in the ozone layer, the increasing changes on the surface of the sun, the sun storms with their effect on planet Earth, but also the satellites and spaceships, the increase in storms, tornadoes and hurricanes as "signs from heaven" (compare Luke 21:25-26).

Wickedness and Moral Decline

"And because iniquity [NIV translates this as wickedness] shall abound, the love of many shall wax cold" (Matthew 24:12).

200

Russian author Dostojevski wrote, "Where God is no longer respected, everything is allowed." Biblical ethics have been done away with since the 1960s. This has consequences today for the state, society and legislation. For instance, the results are euthanasia on one hand and abortion on the other. Up to 50 million unborn children are aborted every year. The media has reported that more and more politicians are coming out of the closet. Same-sex marriages and the adoption of children by them have already become socially acceptable in many countries.

Couples who live together outside of marriage are an absolutely normal practice today. Adultery is considered a necessary part of self-realization. Every third marriage ends in divorce.

Sexual perversions of every nature are available for almost all via television and the Internet. Occultism, satanism, drug abuse, crime and anarchy are eating away at our society.

Almost every day the media reports new paedophilia and child abuse cases. Violence is often glorified. It is estimated that on average a 15-year old child has already seen the violent destruction of over 13,000 human beings on television.

According to official statistics from the German police, 20,000 children are abused annually in Germany. The actual number is probably a lot higher.[21]

The head of the police in Houston said: "Fear of crime is paralyzing American society. We have allowed ourselves to degenerate to such an extent that we live like animals. We live behind bars, have more and more locks on our doors, install burglar alarms, go to bed with a loaded weapon, and then try to find rest."

The American Medical Chamber declared, "Violence in every form, from murder to violence towards women and children, is health problem number one in the land."

The Apostle Paul revealed to Timothy how it would be in the last days before the return of Jesus: "This know also, that in the last days perilous times shall come. For men shall be lovers of their own selves, covetous, boasters, proud, blasphemers, disobedient to parents, unthankful, unholy, without natural affection, trucebreakers, false accusers, incontinent, fierce, despisers of those that are good, traitors, heady, highminded, lovers of pleasures more than lovers of God" (2 Timothy 3:1-4).

People have time for discos, cinemas and parties, but they have no time to go to church. Christians organize their vacations down to the finest detail, but not a few of them leave their Bibles at home. They have time for everything, but not for God

The Destruction of Love

"Because iniquity shall abound, the love of many shall wax cold" (Matthew 24:12).

The further we depart from God, the further we depart from love. Marriage partners are lonely; children are growing up without parental care and supervision. Behavior in society is becoming more and more aggressive.

In Germany up to 50,000 children and young people have left their homes and prefer a life on the streets.

Christian parents are also among those who are affected by this behavior. In Luke 12:53 it says, "The father shall be divided against the son, and the son against the father; the mother against the daughter, and the daughter against the mother; the mother in law against her daughter in law, and the daughter in law against her mother in law."

Natural affection is disintegrating, and people's hearts are growing colder. The natural affection of people and their consciences is being destroyed.

Everyone is out for himself. An increasing selfishness is also perceptible in Israel leading one person to say, "We urgently need a new war to bring us back together!"

German philosopher, Peter Sloterdijk, speaks about a "spherical catastrophe" in our day. Never in the history of mankind has its characteristics been so destroyed as they are today: dualism, the roles of men and women. Divorce rates are explosive. The reason for this is that man is concentrating more and more on himself. Psychologists speak about a "lust totalitarianism." [23]

The Gospel is Reaching all Nations

"And this gospel of the kingdom shall be preached in all the world for a witness unto all nations; and then shall the end come" (Matthew 24:14).

Although the two witnesses or the 144,000 sealed will preach the "gospel of the kingdom," and concerns the coming kingdom of the Messiah, we may also apply it to the preaching of the Gospel today.

All nations have been reached with the Gospel. Dr. Roger Liebi explains that the Greek word for "nations" (*ethnos*) means the "greatest social union." The nation is more than the family, the clan, the tribe and the people.

Since the 18th century, the Bible, which had been translated into 70 languages at that time, has now been translated into more than 2,300 languages. Parts of the Bible are available in significantly more languages. The Gospel has been spread to all countries through literature, radio, television and the Internet.

Finally

Somebody said with regard to our time, "The world is like a tree on which almost all the fruit is ripe. The day of the harvest seems to be near."

The Lord Jesus calls for three things in His endtime message:

1. "But take ye heed: behold, I have foretold you all things" (Mark 13:23).

2. "And he spake to them a parable; Behold the fig tree, and all the trees; when they now shoot forth, ye see and know of your own selves that summer is now nigh at hand" (Luke 21:29-31).

3. "And when these things begin to come to pass, then look up, and lift up your heads; for your redemption draweth nigh" (Luke 21:28).

Peter Hahne said, "In a world of bad news, the message of the Bible is **the** good news."

The good news for our time is that Jesus is coming! That is why it is important to take these words to heart, "Believe on the Lord Jesus Christ, and thou shalt be saved, and thy house" (Acts 16:31). Christ, and to those who have already accepted salvation in Jesus Christ, Colossians 1:13 says, "Who hath delivered us from the power of darkness, and hath translated us into the kingdom of his dear Son."

1. *Entscheidung*
2. *Israel heute*
3. *Factum*
4. Rainer Wagner, Arbeitsbuch-Heilsplan-Glaubenslehre
5. *Der Spiegel*
6. *Facts*
7. *Facts*
8. *EDU Standpunkt*
9. *Idea Spektrum*
10. Report of the WHO in Die Welt
11. *Welt.DE / Der Spiegel*
12. Rainer Wagner, Arbeitsbuch-Heilsplan-Glaubenslehre
13. *Factum*
14. *Factum*
15. *Die Wegweisung*
16. *Idea Spektrum*
17. *Idea Spektrum*
18. Hayne, Michael Drosnin, *Der Countdown*
19. *Idea Spektrum*
20. *Facts*
21. *Dennoch*
22. *Idea Spektrum*
23. *Idea Spektrum*